ROSA CONCORDIAE·SIGNUM

ELIZABETH
OUR QUEEN

Presentation Edition

ELIZABETH
OUR QUEEN

Richard Dimbleby

UNIVERSITY OF LONDON PRESS Ltd.

WARWICK SQUARE, LONDON, E.C.4

Printed in Great Britain for UNIVERSITY OF LONDON PRESS, LTD.,
by Richard Clay and Company, Ltd., Bungay, Suffolk

CONTENTS

INTRODUCTION

MANY books have been written that tell the life-story of Her Majesty the Queen; many others, no doubt, are being prepared. They trace, with pictures and a wealth of anecdote, her life from earliest childhood to the present day. Because there is a limit to the number of true stories of Her Majesty's youth and upbringing which are known to writers, there is a similarity among many of these biographies; the same revealing, often amusing, tales appear in slightly differing form. An accurate life-story, after all, can only be told once; thenceforth all other accounts are but variations of the original.

Therefore I have not presumed to write a biography, or " intimate " story, of Her Majesty. Instead, I have tried to tell her story against its splendid background, relating it always to the significance of the monarchy. This is, if you like, a book about the Sovereign, rather than a book about Queen Elizabeth. It gives some account of the Protestant Succession which put the second Elizabeth on the throne. It describes the careful, arduous training that a future queen must undergo, and it attempts to show the significance of the Sovereign in the life of Britain and the Commonwealth today.

Though the reader will find no gossip and little anecdote in this book, I would not like him or her to read it without having clearly in mind a picture of the woman herself who now bears the heavy burden of queenship and who faces the historic ordeal of Coronation. To most of us, the Queen is a remote person, seen only occasionally in short flashes of pageantry. The clattering of hooves, the sunshine glinting on a State landau, the scarlet-coated postilions, the sudden notes of the National Anthem, and the Queen has come and gone. Those who were lucky saw her smile and wave across the heads of the crowd; those who were not saw her reflection in a mirror held aloft on a stick or hurriedly snatched from a handbag. Some did not see her at all, but felt the surge of excitement and heard the burst of cheers and clapping as she passed.

How different for the Queen, whose whole public life must be lived in front of crowds, troops, dignitaries and cameras. The spontaneous applause that rises and falls as she passes is an unbroken sound in her ears, for cheering keeps pace with the Royal carriage. Wherever she goes, the music of the anthem is with her; troops are always motionless at attention; people about her always formal and correct. Everything she does is watched, everything she wears is noted, everything she says treasured and remembered.

It is a tremendous strain that the Throne imposes upon one person. Helped as she is by her husband's presence, there is much that the Queen must do alone, and do with grace and charm. Those who have the opportunity of seeing Her Majesty at close quarters, as I have done, know how well she exercises those important qualities. They know, too, how suddenly she can switch from one mood to another, not necessarily because an occasion demands it, but because she has a great sense of humour that lies just below the surface, waiting to break through solemnity whenever it can. Photographs rarely do her justice; she is smaller, slimmer, and altogether more lively than they make her. She has a flashing smile that can cut right through the barrier of formality, and a clear, incisive voice. She has, also, a sureness and determination, undoubtedly the result of the years of training, which leave no doubt of her intention and ability to uphold the full authority of the Throne.

I remember watching from a few yards away when Her Majesty made her first appearance after her father's death to distribute the Royal Maundy in Westminster Abbey.

With strict formality, she was conducted along the lines of men and women waiting to receive alms. Everyone in the great nave of the Abbey who was in a position to see the Queen was watching her, a small figure in black, walking between the taller and splendidly robed officers of the Almonry, the Bishop of Lichfield and the Dean of Westminster. They saw her pass along the line, smiling at each old man and woman as she handed them their purse of silver coins. It was a formal ceremony, one that had changed much since its origin nineteen hundred years ago in the Last Supper. Today, in its abbreviated form, it could have been a quick routine occasion. Not so, however, with the Queen. She paused and made a separate ceremony of the handing-over of each bag of alms. At last she came to a group of half a dozen men and women who were blind, and who waited nervously, listening to the footsteps of the Queen and the almoners as they approached.

They need not have been uneasy, for Her Majesty looked at them swiftly and, without prompting, took hold of the hand of the first woman, spoke to her, lifted the hand, and laid a purse in it. She clasped the hand for a moment between her own hands before moving on.

This may seem a small incident to relate, but it is indicative of the quick sympathy and the willingness to depart suddenly from strict formality that the Queen possesses. While intent on maintaining the true and necessary dignity of the Throne, she is quickly responsive to the mood of every occasion.

As you read this account of the history and significance of the Sovereign, therefore, keep in your mind the picture of an intelligent, alert woman who, burdened by the duty of which she has such a deep sense, has kept in her womanhood all the sense of fun and humour that she possessed as a girl.

A new era for Britain opened in February 1952, when the second Elizabeth came to the throne. No more devoted or courageous person than she could carry on the monarchy which is the enduring strength of Britain and the wonder and envy of a large part of the world.

PROLOGUE

FROM Capetown, South Africa, on the evening of April 21, 1947, the voice of Princess Elizabeth travelled across the world. For the celebration of her twenty-first birthday the Princess was six thousand miles from the country of her birth; but, as she said, she was not six thousand miles from home. As heiress presumptive to the throne, she had her home wherever the peoples of the British Commonwealth dwelt. With this broadcast she entered into the lives of those peoples; peoples who within five years were to become her subjects.

Seven years previously, in 1940, at the beginning of the long war with Germany, she had broadcast to the children of the Empire. As a child herself she had spoken as the children's representative and leader.

" When peace comes," said the young Princess on that occasion, "remember it will be for us, the children of today, to make the world of tomorrow a better and happier place."

For those same children, when peace had returned, Princess Elizabeth spoke again as representative on her twenty-first birthday.

" Now that we are coming to manhood and womanhood," she said, " it is surely a great joy to us all to think that we shall be able to take some of the burden off the shoulders of our elders who have fought and worked and suffered to protect our childhood. We must not be daunted by the anxieties and hardships that the war has left behind for every nation of our Commonwealth.

" To make of this ancient Commonwealth which we all love so dearly an even grander thing—more free, more prosperous, more happy, and a more powerful influence for good in the world—we must give nothing less than the whole of ourselves.

" There is a motto which has been borne by many of my ancestors—a noble motto : ' I Serve '. Those words were an inspiration to many bygone heirs to the throne when they made their knightly dedication as they came to manhood. I cannot do quite as they did, but I can do what was not possible for any of them. I can make my solemn act of dedication with a whole Empire listening. I should like to make that dedication now. It is very simple :

> " I declare before you all that my whole life, whether it be long or short, shall be devoted to your service and the service of our great imperial family to which we all belong, but I shall not have the strength to carry out this resolution unless you join in it with me, as I now invite you to do.

" God help me to make good my vow, and God bless all of you who are willing to share it."

PART I

BIRTHRIGHT

CHAPTER I

CHILDHOOD

WHEN making her dedication, Princess Elizabeth was fully aware of the changes that time had wrought in the system of English monarchy.

In Anglo-Saxon times the king was elected by the Witan, which was the Great Council of the nation. Later, much later, in our turbulent history, the government of the nation passed into the hands of the people. When English monarchy was restored in 1660, Charles II came to a throne stripped of many of its powers : Parliament had summoned the monarch, instead of the monarch summoning parliament. In matters of law and finance the king could act only through parliament; he could no longer directly impose taxation or proceed against a subject.

The duties and the responsibilities of monarchy had indeed changed, but in many ways they had become more arduous and exacting than ever before.

Twenty-six years ago, when our Queen became the first Royal infant to be baptised in the private chapel of Buckingham Palace, there was no sign to indicate the destiny that awaited her. King George V, her grandfather, was consolidating the position of the Crown as the head of a family at a time when monarchy throughout Europe was at a discount. Though Britain herself was seething with internal unrest that during the first month of Princess Elizabeth's life was to flare up into the General Strike, it was directed at neither king nor kingship. Rather the Crown was gaining new power out of internal discord.

The value of a monarch above politics to watch like a kindly impartial father over the conflicting elements of his family, and to see that the true will of the electorate prevailed, was becoming more and more widely recognised.

The Prince of Wales (later to become Duke of Windsor), then thirty-two years old, was one of the most popular heirs to the throne of all time. The freedom and informality with which he travelled the world and mixed with the people at large were already being heralded with high hopes. The mantle of monarchy seemed far removed from both the baby Princess and her father, the Duke of York, who had been brought up, as a younger son, to support his brother and remain in the background. With that position the Duke of York was undoubtedly content.

A natural reserve and a slight stammer were no great handicaps in a supporting rôle which, although it called for a share of Royal duties, allowed him his vocation of the sea, his own choice of public service in boys' clubs and the summer camp where he brought rich and poor together in one brotherhood, and the life of a country squire between times.

It was as the daughter of a country gentleman, therefore, that Princess Elizabeth's upbringing began.

Like most children, Princess Elizabeth shared her childhood visits between her respective grandparents.

In her mother's home at Glamis, where her sister Princess Margaret was born, the future Queen played against the romantic background of Scottish history.

The first awareness of monarchy must have been puzzling to the young Princess. Here was the King, treated by all with homage and respect, though the child knew he was really a benevolent grandfather ready to play and to pamper her, and not in the least frightening or awe-inspiring. The love between them was deep and real, and it was the three-years-old Princess who was sent, with medical approval, to cheer and inspire King George V's recovery from his long illness of 1928–29.

One hour with his grand-daughter, King George is reported to have declared, did him more good than all the medicine the royal physicians could prescribe. When, restored to reign for another seven years, he returned from Bognor and appeared on the balcony of Buckingham Palace to acknowledge the sympathy and rejoicing of his people, Princess Elizabeth was at his side, making her first public appearance, waving and blowing kisses to the crowd.

Outside her parents, the influence of Queen Mary played a great part in shaping the character of the future Queen. Queen Victoria had made up her mind that her god-daughter, the Princess Mary of Teck, was one day to be Queen. When she did indeed come to the Throne as the wife of George V, Queen Mary was moulded in her godmother's views on both the Crown and the place of women in public life. Nothing must be done to divert the spotlight from the sovereign.

Whatever her station, a woman's place was in the background supporting her husband. Queen Mary established a pattern for both regal queenliness and dignified womanhood, and she has always lived up to it.

As Queen Consort, Queen Mother, and now Queen Grandmother, she has been most particular about emphasising the precedence of the Crown, no matter upon whose head it rests. When, on her father's death, Queen Elizabeth flew back from Nairobi, a letter from Queen Mary awaited her at the airport. It was signed "Your loving grandmother and subject."

In public life, whatever had to be done, Queen Mary did swiftly and to the point. On one occasion, in a brief talk to a party of children from Dr. Barnardo's Homes who were emigrating to Australia, she gave them her code for living.

"Remember," Queen Mary said, "that life is made up of loyalty. Loyalty to your friends; loyalty to things beautiful and good; loyalty to the country in which you live; loyalty to your King; and, above all—for this holds all other loyalties together—loyalty to God."

That code sums up her influence upon a young Princess who within two dramatic years was to have the meaning of the Throne thrust vividly upon her.

It was in December, 1936, that her father, hitherto the Duke of York, became King George VI, following the abdication of his elder brother, Edward VIII. This was a sudden, unexpected turn of events; and, at the age of ten years and eight months, Princess Elizabeth had become heiress presumptive to the throne.

On her thirteenth birthday, in April 1939, Princess Elizabeth is ready to go for a ride at Windsor.

CHAPTER 2

"KING OF THIS REALM"

FOR the first time in history both the queen
mother and the heiress to the throne were
present at the crowning of a sovereign. There
had been doubt whether Queen Mary would attend
her son's coronation, as it was not the usual custom
for the queen mother to be present; but, knowing the
deep affection in which she was held, King George VI
decided not only upon her attendance but also that she
should have her own procession into Westminster
Abbey.

Separated from their parents and in the care of
their aunt, the Princess Royal, Princess Elizabeth
and her sister had driven in their own coach to
Westminster, and led the procession of the Princes
and Princesses of the Blood Royal into the Abbey.
They had watched the majestic entry of Queen Mary
and her retinue, and had followed their grandmother
into the royal box at the side of the high altar.
Perhaps already conscious of her newly-elevated
position and the dignity it demanded, the eleven-
years-old heiress presumptive tried hard not to be
drawn into the whisperings of her younger sister, who
in her excitement nearly lost her robe of purple
velvet.

The trumpets sounded a fanfare and into the colour-
ful scene came the magnificent spectacle of the royal
procession—the high dignitaries of the Church and

*The scene in Westminster Abbey, as King
George VI is about to be crowned.*

their gleaming crosses, the proud standards of the United Kingdom and Empire, the Royal Standard, and then the Queen, greeted by shouts of " Vivat Regina Elizabetha ". Following came the King's Regalia : high-ranking officers of the three Services bearing the Sword of the Defender of the Faith, the sharp-pointed Sword of Justice and the blunted Sword of Mercy. Then Princess Elizabeth saw her father himself, clad in the long, ermine-edged, crimson robe of State. From the King's Scholars of Westminster School soared the triumphant acclaim: "Vivat, vivat, Rex Georgius ".

When, sixteen years later, the royal procession next entered the Abbey, the Princess, herself, would be the principal in the centuries-old ceremonial, and the Westminster schoolboys traditionally acclaiming her on behalf of the people would once again be Queen's Scholars, the forty Queen's Scholars for whom the first Queen Elizabeth founded the school, saying in her Charter of Incorporation : " The Lord pour forth His spirit upon you, that this our College from age to age may bring forth fruits of holiness and learning, ripe and abundant."

As in the days of the Witan, the king owed his throne to election, so today in the twentieth century the sovereign is still presented to the people that they may show their recognition and " good liking ". Thus in his turn King George VI faced first east, then south, west and north, while four times the Archbishop of Canterbury proclaimed in a loud voice :

" Sirs, I here present unto you King George, your undoubted King. Wherefore all you who are come this day to do your homage and service, are you willing to do the same ? "

Each time back echoed the loud and joyful acclamation : " God Save King George the Sixth ! " The people had shown their willingness, and wished the coronation of their new King to proceed.

By the Coronation Oath—the Triple Oath that remains little changed from the days of the Saxons, and by which the second Queen Elizabeth would also reaffirm her dedication to service—King George VI bound himself by contract with his peoples. Solemnly he swore to govern them, in whatever part of the Commonwealth they lived, according to their respective laws and customs; to do his utmost to cause law and justice, in mercy, to be executed in all his judgments; and to maintain the laws of God, the true profession of the Gospel, the Protestant Reformed Religion in the United Kingdom, the Settlement of the Church of England, and the rights and privileges of Church and clergy.

It is not only through the laws of the realm which establish him on the throne that the king reigns, but also by the grace of God. The king is both knight and priest. And so after the preparatory Communion Service with the same Gospel reading from St. Matthew that has been heard by our Kings and Queens for over a thousand years—the verses containing that immortal reply : " Render unto Cæsar the things that are Cæsar's, and unto God the things that are God's "—the Coronation ceremony moved from the earthly to the spiritual.

Divested of his royal robes, and in a simple white shirt and breeches, King George VI with true humility took his seat on St. Edward's Chair, hewn out of English oak in the fourteenth century. Above his head a canopy of gold was stretched by four Knights of the Garter. Princess Elizabeth saw the mystical anointing of her father, as once Solomon was anointed king by Zadok the priest and Nathan the prophet. On King George VI's hands, his breast, the crown of his head, the Archbishop of Canterbury inscribed the figure of the Cross with consecrated oil from the golden Ampulla, fashioned in the form of an eagle.

To mark his consecrated state, the King was first robed with the counterparts of the garments of priesthood before being invested with the insignia of sovereignty. Then his knighthood was recognised. His heels were touched with the Golden Spurs of St. George, emblem of chivalry. By rights he should have been girt with the Sword of State, which signifies justice, the protection of the Church, the defence of widows and orphans, and the punishment of wrongdoing and the reformation of what is amiss; but the two-handed, double-edged Sword of State is too massive to be girt about any man's waist. In its place, therefore, the Lord Great Chamberlain fixed to the King's golden belt the smaller Sword of Offering.

Rising, the King ungirded the sword and, bearing it flat in his two hands, carried it to the High Altar into the keeping of God. However, as this Sword of Offering was a substitute for the Sword of State, and consequently an earthly belonging of the King and not a relic of the regalia, it was redeemed upon payment of one hundred shillings by the Marquess of Zetland, who had previously borne the Sword of State. Thereafter the Marquess carried instead the unsheathed Sword of Offering.

The Imperial Robe, a mantle of gold embroidered with roses, was buckled across the King's chest. The richly jewelled Orb surmounted by a cross, symbol of Christ's dominion over the world, was placed in the King's hands by the Archbishop, who then placed on the fourth finger of his right hand the King's Ring, emblem of kingly dignity and the defence of the Christian faith. With that ring the Sovereign becomes virtually wedded to the nation.

Now came the Archbishop with two golden rods, the Sceptre with the Cross, from which shone the " Great Star of Africa " stone cut from the Cullinan diamond ; and the Sceptre topped with the image of a dove, symbol of equity and mercy.

" Receive the Royal Sceptre, the ensign of kingly power and justice," said the Archbishop, passing the Sceptre with the cross into the King's right hand. He then delivered into the King's left hand the Sceptre with the dove with the injunction : " Be so merciful that you be not too remiss ; so execute justice that you forget not mercy. Punish the wicked, protect and cherish the just, and lead your people in the way wherein they should go."

To an eleven-year-old Princess, no matter how well she may have been primed by her grandmother or aunt in the ancient rites of the ceremonial, the moment, thrilling above all, that she and her sister must have been awaiting was the self-explanatory climax of the service : the moment when she saw the Archbishop of Canterbury raise aloft the Crown of England. As the Crown was lowered on to her father's head a thousand voices in the Abbey acclaimed him with the cry, " God Save the King ! " A cry that at once sped round the world as silver trumpets, rolling drums, saluting guns and pealing bells heralded the news that a new sovereign had been crowned.

One more presentation to the King remained, the gift of the Bible—" the most valuable thing that this world affords : wisdom, royal law, and the lively oracles of God "—before he was lifted on to the Throne to assume his kingdom.   The drums rolled, the trumpets sounded their fanfare, and the Westminster Scholars, in their traditional rôle of the people, led the congregation in the Biblical salutation :

> " God Save King George !
> Long Live King George !
> May the King Live for Ever ! "

After the lords spiritual and temporal had paid homage to their new Sovereign, the ceremonial anointing and crowning of the Queen Consort followed; and, as the Archbishop placed upon Queen Elizabeth's head the " Crown of glory, honour and joy " from which sparkled the famous Kohinoor diamond, so Princess Elizabeth, Heiress Presumptive, together with the peeresses, put on her coronet—a golden circlet lightweight when compared with the Crown of England, St. Edward's Crown, that would next be placed upon her head in Westminster Abbey.   This must not be confused with the Imperial State Crown, which is studded with sapphires, rubies, and diamonds, and is worn on State occasions.   St. Edward's Crown is used only for the Coronation Service.   It is a circlet of gold with four crosses alternating with fleurs-de-lys, on a cap of crimson velvet, surmounted with the Orb and Cross, and weighs five pounds.   It is a " Crown of pure gold " : a " Crown of glory and righteousness ".

PART II

TRAINING FOR THE THRONE

CHAPTER 3

CONSTANT PURPOSE

THE word " monarchy " is derived from two Greek words meaning " rule alone ". From the start, however, King George VI was far from being alone.

As the nation depended for stability and greatness upon a strong, moral family life, so, too, the throne settled down securely upon the firm foundation of family unity and strength. It was " the Queen and I " who pledged themselves to national service and prayed God for guidance and strength to follow the path that lay before them; and when the time came for Princess Elizabeth to begin making speeches, the words " my father " instinctively followed any reference to the King.

" The King, my father." Though home was now a palace, much more important was the fact that the palace was a home in the true christian meaning of the word, although duties of State robbed the King and Queen of many hours that they would have liked to spend with their children.

To King George VI and Queen Elizabeth now fell also the task of bringing up not only a daughter but a future sovereign. True, Princess Elizabeth was simply heiress presumptive, but the possibility of a male heir was becoming remote. As parents, both the King and Queen naturally wished to continue the policy they had established as Duke and Duchess of York, of shielding their daughter from too much limelight.

Gradually, however, Princess Elizabeth was introduced to public life. Naturally, she began with youth movements and interests. She became a girl guide in Buckingham Palace's own Company; and at twelve she became president of the Children's League of the Princess Elizabeth of York Hospital in the East End of London.

Her education was planned to include many subjects not normally found in any school curriculum. In particular, she made a special study of the constitutional history of our country; that is, of the growth and form of its methods of government, and of the nation's way of life. She studied in great detail the way in which our monarchy had developed. Important, too, was a sound knowledge of the histories of the Commonwealth. Later it was thought that a future sovereign should also learn about the affairs of our chief partner in the democratic way of life. Princess Elizabeth thus became the first heir to the throne to read American history.

The staff of tutors to the Princess grew. She was taught French and German, and Canon Crawley of St. George's Chapel, Windsor, was made responsible for both religious instruction and studies in scriptural history.

Sir Henry Marten, then vice-provost of Eton, was

selected as Princess Elizabeth's chief tutor, particularly in the various fields of history. " To have a mind capable of mastering things is far more important than the knowledge you actually get," Sir Henry once said. He gave his first impression of his important charge as " a somewhat shy girl of thirteen who when asked a question would look for confidence and support to her governess—an unnecessary action as I thought, because the answer was almost invariably correct ".

Meanwhile, with the King and Queen away on the royal tour of Canada in the spring of 1939, Queen Mary, in whose care the Princess was left, took a hand in shaping her practical education. It was not enough, Queen Mary considered, for a future queen to read about the treasures and institutions of the national heritage : she must see them for herself. Accordingly Princess Elizabeth and her sister were taken on a series of informal visits to museums, art galleries, and such historic buildings as the Tower of London.

As Princess Elizabeth grew older, the scope of her practical education broadened. She took in her stride commercial institutions, factories, workshops, the Bank of England, and the Royal Mint, seeing how things were done and meeting the people who did them.

In the House of Commons she listened to the making of the laws of the country, the laws by which her own sovereignty would be established, the laws through which the people themselves consented to be governed, the laws of the constitution that she would solemnly vow to uphold. In the Courts of Justice she saw the same law in operation—" law and justice in mercy being executed in all judgments ". Again, these were no visits specially prepared beforehand. Just as the Princess had mingled unnoticed with everyday passengers on underground and bus, so she arrived unheralded in Court. In the view of her parents this was an advantage rather than an embarrassment. Their wish was always for their daughter to gain first-hand knowledge of affairs as they were, not as they appeared through rose-tinted spectacles.

Whatever the situation or crisis that their daughter might meet, they were happy in the knowledge that she would be able to face it with the moral strength and character derived from a good home life and a united family, a blessing to which she was to pay many tributes later in her public speeches.

" It has become unfashionable to believe in fixed standards of morality, even if those standards have stood the test of nearly two thousand years," Princess Elizabeth told the people of Wales when she accepted the Freedom of Cardiff in 1948. " We cannot then blame children whose upbringing in some cases hardly gives them a chance to know the difference between right and wrong. It is so often conditions at home which are responsible. I myself have been extremely lucky in this respect and I can speak with feeling of the advantages which a happy family life brings to a child."

Both Queen Victoria and King Edward VII and, to a lesser degree, King George V had brought up their children on the Victorian theory that strength of character could only be fashioned by severity and repression. But there was nothing severe about Princess Elizabeth's upbringing. Her character was developed by " that best of disciplines, founded on respect for what is right, as well as on affection ", and an absence of " foolish spoiling ". It was an upbringing that brought not priggishness but true joy.

" In the days of my childhood ", Princess Elizabeth once remarked, " the sun seemed always to be shining."

CHAPTER 4

THE WAR YEARS

"WE shall fight on the beaches, we shall fight on the landing-grounds, we shall fight in the fields and in the streets, we shall fight in the hills; we shall never surrender."

These inspiring words were spoken by the Prime Minister in 1940, when it seemed likely that Britain would be invaded. At that time, many who had the means to do so sent their children overseas to Canada and the United States. Many people, indeed, thought that Princess Elizabeth and her sister should themselves travel to safety in Canada.

To pressure from all quarters, however, the King and Queen remained firm. They were not in a position, they considered, to allow themselves the indulgence of their feelings and concern as parents. As the "First Family", they were representative of all Britain's families and, knowing that most people had no choice in the matter but had to "stay put", the King and Queen wished to share whatever risks other families might have to run. It was therefore at Windsor, in strict secrecy, that the Princesses spent the greater part of the war.

To many, the war brought new surroundings, new acquaintances, new comradeships. To Princess Elizabeth it gave an opportunity of meeting and mixing with her future subjects on a scale that might not otherwise have been possible.

With her sister, Margaret, she joined evacuee children in village concerts in aid of the comforts funds for the forces. This spurred Princess Elizabeth's interest in amateur theatricals to greater efforts, out of which sprang first a nativity play and then the famous Windsor pantomimes that became a feature of the royal family's wartime Christmases. Her repertoire expanded to include singing, dancing, dramatic recitations, and ukulele-playing.

The Princess became active, too, in the Sea Rangers Amateur Theatrical Society. The King was invited to one production that she had organised; and Princess Elizabeth must have known all the worries suffered by children over parents' appearance and deportment at school functions, for Princess Margaret was sent with a message asking the King to be sure to attend in naval uniform, as the concert was " a naval occasion ".

As the war went on, the Princess became the link between the children of all the nations of the British Commonwealth. In October 1940 the thirteen-and-a-half-year-old Princess broadcast in the Children's Hour to the children of the Commonwealth. She spoke with moving sincerity and a marked singleness of purpose.

The young heiress presumptive was preparing for the destiny that lay ahead. Before a man or woman could make a good sovereign he or she must first be a good citizen, and it was through youth movements that Princess Elizabeth learned in practice the elements of citizenship. On her own initiative she had joined the Girl Guides, a movement that she herself later described as " bounded by no narrow prejudice of race, class, or creed, but one seeking to join all together in friendship, based on a common promise and upon a common attempt to order their lives in accordance with the laws of the movement ".

She had no greater help in keeping to those laws, or becoming proficient in guide activities, than any other girl of her age.   In fact, so far as some of the practical activities were concerned, her position put her at a distinct disadvantage.   Her guide captain recalls that the Princess, then fourteen, found considerable difficulty in passing the first-class test.

" The Cook, Needlewoman and Child Nurse are holding me up a bit, but I hope to pass soon," Princess Elizabeth explained, and added, ruefully, " I think I have forgotten how to sweep a room now."

Years later Princess Elizabeth was to speak from personal knowledge of the difficulty of living always to the ideal of the movement.   She addressed a conference of rangers at Girl Guide Headquarters, saying :

" The promise and laws are simple and anyone can understand them ; but that does not make them easy to fulfil.   On the contrary, they are difficult.   They demand faith, honesty, self-control, and love for our neighbours.   The demand that rangers should hold to these high principles comes at one of the most difficult periods of their lives.

" Life today is a struggle.   Rangers, in accepting their promise and the law, take upon themselves an extra struggle.   They have to sacrifice themselves and keep their high ideals.   If they do this successfully they will be greatly strengthened in a world that is full of materialism, dishonesty, and devotion to self."

With the approach of her sixteenth birthday hopes began to be expressed that Princess Elizabeth would be created Princess of Wales. It was a wish that was to gain increasing support in the next two years.

Since 1301, when Edward I gave his young son born in Carnarvon Castle the title of " Prince of Wales " (thereby, according to a popular legend, keeping a promise to give the Welsh people a prince who " could speak no word of English "—a legend which takes no notice of the fact that the lad was already seventeen) the title has been conferred upon the sovereign's eldest son. The eldest son—the Heir Apparent—is automatically Duke of Cornwall by birth, but it is necessary for him to be created Prince of Wales. But by reason of her sex, Princess Elizabeth could never be Heir Apparent. She was Heiress Presumptive; that is, it was presumed that she would succeed to the throne provided her father did not have a son.

Nevertheless, to many it seemed pointless not to give Wales a royal leader in this way. British monarchy, however, thinks not in terms of ten or twenty years, but in generations. A precedent now might be an embarrassment in years to come, and so from Buckingham Palace on February 11, 1944, came the announcement that " His Majesty the King does not contemplate making any change in the style and title of the Princess Elizabeth on the occasion of her approaching eighteenth birthday ".

It was no doubt in sympathy with the popular viewpoint, however, that King George VI chose South Wales as the first area to which Princess Elizabeth should accompany him and the Queen on an official tour; and the people of Wales made up for any disappointment at the lack of the official title by hailing her unofficially as "*Ein Tywysoges*" (Our own Princess).

On March 28, 1942, Princess Elizabeth was confirmed by the Archbishop of Canterbury in the private chapel of Windsor Castle. She was within a month of her sixteenth birthday. Only two years were left before the Princess would have to be ready, if necessary, to assume the Crown and the leadership of her people without notice.

Years before, in one of the first speeches he ever made as Duke of York, her father had spoken of his ideas of leadership. To his mind, the leader needed three great qualities: personality, sympathy, and, above all, idealism.

"I do not think I need speak to you about personality," he said. "Of sympathy I will say just this: its keynote is personal contact and understanding. The third quality of the leader is idealism. Nobody can lead unless he has the gift of vision, and the desire in his soul to leave things in the world a little better than he found them. He will strive for something which may be unattainable, but which he believes in his heart can one day be reached. If not by him, by his successors, if he can help pave the way."

King George VI had striven always to develop personality and idealism in his daughter by her daily routine of living, by her solid family atmosphere, by his own example, by his " helping to pave the way for his successors "—in particular, his daughter—towards the goal of a better life in a better world.

It was time now to begin the personal contact of

Princess Elizabeth broadcasts her twenty-first-birthday speech from Capetown.

future leader and subject, and the development of the quality of understanding and sympathy. As a first step the heiress presumptive was officially introduced to the armed forces by her appointment as Colonel of the Grenadier Guards. The Grenadiers are the first of the five regiments—the others are the Coldstream, and the Scots, Irish and Welsh Guards—which make up the Brigade of Guards. It was the first time in their history that the Grenadiers had a woman as their colonel.

In addition to reviewing her Grenadiers and receiving from them the present of a diamond brooch in the form of the regimental badge, Princess Elizabeth had one other public duty to perform on her sixteenth birthday—the duty that fell to all of her age, no matter how high or humble their birth. In girl guide uniform she attended at the Windsor Employment Exchange and registered in the normal way as a private citizen for national service. Her one desire was to enlist as quickly as possible.

Both King and Cabinet, however, considered that uninterrupted training for the throne was her most vital form of national service. It was not a decision that the Princess found easy to accept, and she tried hard to have it changed.

It would be she who would one day lead the young people of her own age in the rebuilding of peace and the shaping of the future. To share the same war-time experiences as girls of her own age would, she

Above : *The Royal Family, with Field-Marshal Smuts, in Natal National Park during the tour of South Africa.*

Below : *During their visit to Ottawa, Princess Elizabeth and the Duke of Edinburgh went to Lansdowne Park, where thousands of boys and girls waited to greet them.*

considered, greatly help her understanding of her future subjects and their problems.

It was this argument no doubt that led to the reversal of the original decision. On March 4, 1945, it was announced that :

" The King has granted Her Royal Highness the Princess Elizabeth a commission with the honorary rank of second subaltern in the Auxiliary Territorial Service [now the W.R.A.C.—Women's Royal Army Corps].   Her Royal Highness is at present attending a course at a driving training centre in the south of England."

As a result, at the A.T.S. Mechanical Transport Training Centre near Camberley, King's daughter and Colonel of the Grenadier Guards was entered in the records as " No. 230873 Second Subaltern Elizabeth Alexandra Mary Windsor. Age 18. Eyes, blue. Hair, brown. Height 5 ft. 3 in. National Registration Number : SWGC 55/1/."

There, on the instructions of the King and at her own personal wish, Princess Elizabeth was treated exactly the same as any other trainee of second subaltern rank. In addition to studying military law and administration she learned the Service method of driving and maintaining small cars, heavy lorries, and ambulances.

The training report on the newly-qualified royal transport officer stated : " Extremely quick to learn. She is not rash, and drives with consideration and thought for others on the road, and with every care for her car."

CHAPTER 5

"I SERVE"

MUCH as Princess Elizabeth may have liked to do so, it was not possible for her to remain in the A.T.S. The nation as a whole wanted to see her; and it was important that she should have more personal contact with people both in support of her father and in training for her future queenship. The period of service in the A.T.S. had to be limited. Once its purpose had been accomplished, the heiress presumptive could no longer be spared from state duties. Refreshed by the complete change that the A.T.S. life had given her, she returned to public life on an increasing scale.

Between May 1944, when she made her first public speech, and her enlistment in the A.T.S., Princess Elizabeth fulfilled some dozen or so official engagements by herself.

The most important of these was the launching on December 1, 1944, of Britain's biggest battleship, H.M.S. *Vanguard*. For the first time Princess Elizabeth's own standard was broken from a flagstaff, and it blew out bravely in a bitter December wind over the massed crowds of Clydeside shipbuilders and their families and neighbours, On the way to the platform one of the officials in the party commented on the cold weather, but the Princess replied : " I'm too nervous to notice it."

There was nothing nervous, however, about the

ringing tones in which she proclaimed : " I name this ship *Vanguard*. God bless her and all who sail in her."

The bottle of Empire wine shattered against the prow in the ritual christening, but the ship remained motionless. Between the pressing of the button operating the launching mechanism and the movement of the ship there was a time-lag of several seconds, and for a moment the eighteen-years-old Princess showed a glimpse of her inward nervousness.

" Oh dear," she whispered to Mr. A. V. Alexander, then First Lord of the Admiralty, " she isn't going to move."

Her concern was needless, however. Almost as she expressed her fear, the ship slid slowly down the slipway into the water, to the shouts and cheering of the crowd and the crashing chords of " Rule Britannia ", and Princess Elizabeth smiled with relief.

It was natural that prominent among the engagements of those first years of public service should figure matters affecting the younger generation, whose leader Princess Elizabeth was. When the war ended she turned her attention more and more to youth welfare and interests and to inspiring youth to rebuild and plan for the future that would belong to her and to her contemporaries. Never before, she realised, had the country been so much in need of courage and high purpose.

Many of the problems of youth arose from conditions in the home, from homes shattered by war and its consequences, by broken marriages and domestic strife, by lack of discipline and morals, by cruelty and neglect.

She, to whom the words " home " and " family " meant unity and love, strength and security, could not understand how anyone could be cruel to a child.

" To be cruel to a little child is indeed a dreadful crime," she told members of the National Society for the Prevention of Cruelty to Children in 1945. " It is sad to reflect that in these days there should be need for a Society such as ours, but there can be no doubt as to its value to the whole community. Now the war in Europe is won and we can look forward to peace in the future, I trust it will be possible for our Society to devote its full powers to give every child a chance to lead a happy and useful life."

And again she expressed her Society's aim : " A good home life is the rock on which a child's future is founded. It is, therefore, the aim of the Society to keep the family united and to remove, wherever possible, all that might injure children, either mentally or physically."

Constantly the Princess asked the different youth organisations—of which she had had personal experience—to fear not the adventurous path that lay ahead, but to meet it with courage and resourcefulness and make it a path that would lead to a way of peace, new life, and happiness.

The aftermath of war had made apparent the general apathy towards morals and religion. It had brought also a reluctance to criticise this trend, however much one may in one's heart have condemned it. The fashion for scorning the basic principles of our code of living was often too strong for the average citizen, particularly the younger members of the community, to make an open stand against it.

Wise leadership, Princess Elizabeth considered, could ultimately change this outlook. She referred to the subject often, but never more forcibly than in October 1949, when, to a rally of young wives organised by the Mothers' Union, she made a memorable and important speech.

" Some of the very principles on which the family, and therefore the health of the nation, is founded, are in danger," Princess Elizabeth declared. " We live in an age of growing self-indulgence and of falling moral standards. There will always be unhappy marriages, especially when, as in time of war and of housing shortages, it is difficult for people to live normal married lives. But when we see around us the havoc which has been wrought, above all among children, by the break-up of homes, we can have no doubt that divorce and separation are responsible for some of the darkest evils in our society today.

" I do not think you can perform any finer service than to help maintain the Christian doctrine that the relation of husband and wife is a permanent one, not lightly to be broken because of difficulties or quarrels. . . . I believe there is a far greater fear in our generation of being labelled as priggish. In consequence, people are sometimes afraid to show disapproval of what they know to be wrong, and thus they end by seeming to condone what in their hearts they dislike. I am sure that it is just as wrong to err on that side as it is to be intolerant and over-critical."

The same practical outlook marked Princess Elizabeth's approach to post-war conditions generally. If ever people had believed that the end of the war would bring an end to austerity they were quickly disillusioned.   Britain had to start afresh to earn her living and her place amongst the free peoples of the world.   Austerity was, indeed, not only the order of the day, but the outlook for years to come.

The heiress presumptive was unperturbed.   With youthful enthusiasm she sought in austerity itself the challenge against which the nation could match its spirit of adventure.   This was no time for regrets.

In November 1947 she spoke to the Royal Society of Arts.

" It may well be long years before we can again afford to devote such leisure and energy to things purely decorative as did our forefathers," Princess Elizabeth said.   " But we should be unimaginative indeed if we concluded that because nearly everything we produce today must be severely practical it must also be without taste or beauty.

" Great Britain led the world into the industrial revolution.   That was, no doubt, an historic contribution to human progress ; but there has also been a legacy of squalor, misery, and ugliness as well as the fall in standards of taste which accompanied mass production.   In a sense we have a duty to lead the world in finding the remedy.   If we are destined to live in an austere age, it is for us to establish that beauty is an essential to utility."

CHAPTER 6

H. R. H. THE DUKE OF EDINBURGH

IN this way, Princess Elizabeth faced the problems of the day. As for the normal recreations and pleasures of her generation, long before the burden of the Crown descended upon her the Princess realised that any attempt to share in them attracted the eyes of over five hundred million people scattered throughout the British Commonwealth of Nations.

There was, at all times, a great deal of speculation about her private life and about her personal friendships. In particular, there were many guesses—mostly inaccurate—about the identity of her future husband.

It was, of course, natural that people should wonder about the man who might become the husband of their future Queen, but whoever Princess Elizabeth married would never be their King; he would be only husband of the Queen, an entirely domestic rôle with no official rights or powers in the government of the country.

Under the Royal Marriages Act of 1772, no member of the Royal Family, " male or female (other than the issue of Princesses who have married or who may marry into foreign families), shall be capable of contracting matrimony without the previous consent of His Majesty, his heirs, and successors, signified under the Great Seal ".

If the sovereign refuses consent and the Royal person concerned is over twenty-five years of age, then he or she may give notice to the Privy Council, and the marriage may take place after twelve months, provided parliament has not meanwhile expressed disapproval.

On March 18, 1947, among a list of British naturalisations published in the *London Gazette*, appeared the entry: " Mountbatten, Philip; Greece; serving officer in His Majesty's Forces; 16 Chester Street, London, S.W.1." Prince Philip of Greece and Denmark had taken the oath of allegiance on February 28 of that year, and under the normal procedure had abandoned his foreign titles to become Lieutenant Philip Mountbatten, R.N.

He had made his first application for naturalisation in 1939, but before this could go through the second World War intervened and all naturalisation was suspended. At the end of the war, in which he received a Mention in Despatches for his service as a midshipman in H.M.S. *Valiant* at the Battle of Cape Matapan, he availed himself of the priority application for naturalisation available to all aliens who had served with distinction in His Majesty's Forces.

Educated in Britain, he went to the Royal Naval College at Dartmouth, and it was here, where Prince Philip gained the King's Dirk as the best all-round cadet, that he and Princess Elizabeth, who was with her father and mother on a royal visit of inspection, first consciously became acquainted. Thereafter they maintained a correspondence and Prince Philip sometimes spent his wartime leaves at Windsor.

From Buckingham Palace on July 9, 1947, came at last the expected announcement: " It is with the greatest pleasure that the King and Queen announce the betrothal of their dearly beloved daughter the Princess Elizabeth to Lieutenant Philip Mountbatten, R.N., son of the late Prince Andrew of Greece and Princess Andrew (Princess Alice of Battenberg), to which union The King has gladly given his consent.''

There were, of course, criticisms of the engagement. Was such a high-spirited young man, who liked living hard and playing hard, driving at high speed, and taking a home-made boat out in all weathers on somewhat risky trips round the Orkneys, quite a suitable husband for the heiress presumptive? Admirable as such qualities of dash and daring might be in the Navy—in which he had gained promotion to the appointment of first lieutenant in H.M.S. *Wallace* at the age of twenty-one—surely someone more settled and serious would have been a better choice for consort of our future queen? These were the questions that people asked.

Beneath Philip's gaiety and free-and-easy manner, however, lay an unsuspected side of serious thought that was soon revealed in his speeches. It was known that he had refused point-blank to allow all his speeches to be written for him. As a compromise, he had given the assurance that he would say nothing untoward, but beyond that he would not go. If he could not say what he thought in his own words, he would say nothing at all.

It was his presidential address to the meeting of the British Association for the Advancement of Science—once described as the most brilliant collection of brains in the country—that brought a fuller understanding of the extent of the nation's gain in Princess Elizabeth's choice.

He chose his own subject—the history of scientific achievement over the past hundred years—and wrote the speech himself in his cabin in H.M.S. *Magpie* in the Mediterranean after consulting various scientists.

" The instrument of scientific knowledge in our hands," he said, " is growing more powerful every day. Indeed, it has reached a point when we can either set the world free from drudgery, fear, hunger, and pestilence, or obliterate life itself.

" The nation's wealth and prosperity are governed by the use of science in its industries and commerce. The nation's workers depend upon science for the maintenance and improvement in their standard of health, housing, and food.

" It is clearly our duty as citizens to see that science is used for the benefit of mankind. For of what use is science if man does not survive ? "

It was not only his speech and capability that impressed, but also the way in which the royal president mixed with his audience and showed his eagerness to learn from them.

On the eve of the wedding Lieutenant Philip Mountbatten had a private audience at Buckingham Palace with the King. As Philip knelt before his future father-in-law, King George VI touched him on each shoulder with his sword in the ceremonial accolade, and then invested him with the insignia of a Knight Companion of the Most Noble Order of the Garter, the order to which he had but a few days before admitted his daughter, Princess Elizabeth. When Lieutenant Mountbatten rose from his knees he was no longer a commoner, but a royal duke.

" His Majesty has been pleased to authorise the use of the prefix His Royal Highness, by Lieutenant

Mountbatten," said the statement issued from Buckingham Palace, " and to approve that the dignity of a dukedom of the United Kingdom be conferred upon him by the name, style, and title of the Baron Greenwich of Greenwich in the County of London, Earl of Merioneth, and Duke of Edinburgh."

By these three titles the husband of the future Queen was united to each of the countries of Great Britain. The Dukedom of Edinburgh, previously held by Prince Alfred, the second son of Queen Victoria, had originally been bestowed in 1726 upon Frederick Lewis, eldest son of the Prince of Wales (afterwards George II).

The creation of the ancient earldom of Merioneth goes back into the mists of Welsh history. The title was held by one of the princes of Llewellyn the Great, who led the struggle for a Welsh nationalist revival early in the thirteenth century against the feudal Lords Marchers and their private armies.

The barony of Greenwich had been extinct since 1794. Military leader though the previous holder of the barony had been, it is the Royal Navy with which Greenwich, home of the Royal Naval College and the National Maritime Museum, has so long been associated. It was no doubt the desire to pay tribute to the naval services of the Duke, as well as to represent the capital of the United Kingdom in his dignity, that influenced the choice of this title.

CHAPTER 7

ROYAL WEDDING

THE year 1947 had been a black one in British history. The early months had seen the worst blizzards, the worst floods, and the severest winter of the century. There had been a wholesale switch-off of power and a Government-ordered shutdown of industry that for three weeks brought the country to a standstill.

Abroad, our fortunes seemed no happier. Many people feared that other Commonwealth countries would follow India's example and would wish to become independent republics. India made it plain, however, that although she desired a republican status she had no wish to leave the Commonwealth; even though her great-great-grandmother's proud title, "Empress of India", would no longer be inherited by that royal bride of the 20th November, 1947, the Indian people were willing to recognise her as Head of the Commonwealth of which they remained members.

There had been suggestions that the Princess should be married quietly in St. George's Chapel, Windsor, scene of the wedding of King Edward VII. The people, however, wanted to celebrate the royal wedding in all its richness of pomp and dignity, and to forget for a moment the drabness of everyday life.

Seconding the faithful Commons' address of congratulation, Mr. Churchill said :

" There is no doubt that the approaching marriage gives keen and widespread pleasure in British homes, and that it stirs most warm and lively sympathies in the hearts of the British nation.   Our constitutional monarchy and the Royal Family play a vital part in the tradition, dignity, and romance of our island life."

Quoting Shakespeare's " one touch of nature makes the whole world kin ", he added : " Millions will welcome this joyous event as a flash of colour on the hard road we have to travel."

The world loves a wedding, and the world went to the wedding, with republican countries as keenly interested as the world's few remaining kingdoms.

In a dress made of silk from West Cumberland with a train spun from silk-worms at Lullingstone Castle, embroidered with white Roses of York, with orange blossoms, and ears of corn and wheat, emblems of harvest and fertility, Princess Elizabeth drove with her father in the Irish State Coach to Westminster Abbey.   The morning was still overcast, but there was sunlight in the pealing of the bells and the cheering and laughter of the crowds.   The slow, emphatic strains of the National Anthem greeted the arrival of the coach at the West Door.

In my broadcast commentary upon the scene I recorded : " The doors of the coach are open.   The crowd shouts with excitement and love.   The King, in the uniform of Admiral of the Fleet, comes forward to help his daughter alight carefully.   Now she steps down.   A great cheer rises to sustain her.

" She pauses for a moment and looks at the Abbey.

And perhaps—perhaps she is a little nervous in her heart as she passes from the grey of the morning outside into the warmth and colour of the Abbey."

The Princess walked with her father into the presence of history. With the greatness of the past—the bygone kings and queens, the statesmen, the poets, the soldiers; the Unknown Warrior brought from France to lie amongst the most illustrious in the land, symbol of heroism and the supreme sacrifice " for God, for King and country, for loved ones, home and Empire, for the sacred cause of justice and the freedom of the world "—with the greatness of the past as silent witness Elizabeth, the woman, took Philip, the man.

" Notwithstanding the splendour and national significance of the service in this Abbey," said Dr. Garbett, the Archbishop of York, in his address, " it is in all essentials exactly the same as it would be for any cottager who might be married this afternoon in some small country church in a remote village in the Dales. The same vows are taken : the same prayers are offered : the same blessings are given."

The essentials were the same. It was, like all weddings, a family wedding, a wedding in which the whole family of the British Commonwealth of Nations was able to share personally because of King George VI's permission that the royal wedding ceremony should be broadcast. In fact by that miracle of radio the distant branches of the family in Canada and Australia were able to hear Princess Elizabeth's softly-whispered response, " I will ", which escaped all but those nearest the high altar and the shrine of St. Edward the Confessor in the Abbey itself.

So came to an end the simple service, and hand in hand the royal couple proceeded slowly down the aisle. They came out from the Abbey to receive the full impact of crowds and noise and cheering as first the bride, with her long, lovely train, and then the bridegroom stepped into the coach. The horses pranced, the escort of Household Cavalry held itself ready. Then the signal was given, and to the rhythmic accompaniment of clattering hooves the regal glass coach bore the newly-married couple through the crowded streets to Buckingham Palace; to the wedding breakfast at which the King proposed their health—by tradition the sole toast on such an occasion; to crowds to be greeted from the balcony; to more crowds as, with the King and Queen leading the pursuit across the courtyard to shower them with rose-petals, they drove away in an open landau drawn by four grey horses on the first stage of their honeymoon journey.

In February, 1948, Princess Elizabeth had returned to her royal duties, a Princess confident and strengthened in the knowledge that she faced her future destiny with the support and comfort of the man she loved.

Meanwhile, the Duke of Edinburgh had returned to the Navy, not to the sea that he loved, but attached temporarily to the Admiralty and to Greenwich. When Princess Elizabeth had launched the 34,000-ton liner, *Caronia*, in October 1947, she had been accompanied by Philip.

" I am so happy," Princess Elizabeth had said, " that on this my third visit to Clydeside my future husband is by my side."

Now, as her husband, he was to appear regularly at her side on tours that were not only extending the heiress presumptive's own knowledge of her future domain, but training her Consort for the rôle to which love had brought him.

He was with her when she paid her first visit to foreign soil in May 1948, and shared her first practical experience of the international aspect of the Crown. Fittingly her father had chosen as her first training in this respect Paris, capital of the country which little more than a century before had been our traditional enemy, and was now our main partner in maintaining democracy in Europe.

" The contrast between our rivalries and the confidence which our two peoples feel in each other is a striking one. It proves that among nations, as among individuals, the bitterest enmity can give way to friendship just as profound," Princess Elizabeth told the French.

" All men who wish to preserve the value for which you and we have fought two wars side by side, must look well beyond their frontiers. No country is morally self-sufficient, any more than it is economically self-supporting. Therefore we must be ready to throw into a common pool the gifts and virtues which are our most cherished heritage."

The Duke of Edinburgh, too, found that this official visit to France was very different from others he had made before. Their enthusiastic reception by the crowd was far more than a cordial welcome for a charming young couple.

" Part of that welcome may have been for us personally," commented the Duke afterwards. " At any rate we liked to think so. But we are both convinced that the crowds who greeted us were expressing through us their friendship for our country-men. Those waves and cheers expressed the good-will felt by the people of France for the people of this country, and if through us they have been able to see you, we are well satisfied."

On June 8, 1948, the Duke of Edinburgh was made a Freeman of the City of London.

" Since the last war you have taken the oppor-tunity of honouring those men who were principally responsible for the allied victory, all of them great leaders of men, whether in Parliament or in civil life or on the field of battle," the Duke replied in acknowledging the honour. " But in every kind of human activity there are those who lead and those who follow. You have honoured the leaders. Now, if you will allow me, I would like to accept the Free-dom of this City not only for myself but for all those millions who followed during the second World War. Our only distinction is that we did what we were told to do to the very best of our ability, and kept on doing it.

" Good leaders undoubtedly got the best out of us, and without their leadership our efforts would have been fruitless. However, those leaders will not always be with us, and the time will come when members of our generation will have to take their place. In peace as in war the followers have a great contri-bution to make to their country and to the cause of peace in the world generally."

Princess Elizabeth had broadcast her own dedica-tion of service from South Africa on her twenty-first birthday. The Duke ended his speech by confirming his own assumption of a share in that testament.

" The ideal that my wife and I have set before us is to make the utmost use of the special opportunities we have to try to bring home to our own generation the full importance of that contribution and the effort, both at work and at play, that is required of us."

Nearly a year after the royal wedding it was announced from Buckingham Palace that a Prince had been born to Princess Elizabeth. The date was November 14, 1948.

For the first time for more than fifty years a child had been born in direct line of succession to the throne. The booming of forty-one guns—once the only prompt means of notifying such news to the populace —signalled the birth of the royal infant.

Shortly before the birth of the Prince a decision was taken by King George VI by Letters Patent under the Great Seal of the Realm to fix the style and title of the children of the marriage between Princess Elizabeth and the Duke of Edinburgh.

" It is declared by the Letters Patent," announced the *London Gazette* of November 9, 1948, "that the children of the aforesaid marriage shall have, and at all time hold and enjoy the style, title or attribute of Royal Highness and the titular dignity of Prince or Princess prefixed to their respective Christian names in addition to any other appellations and titles of honour which may belong to them thereafter."

As a result Prince Charles will become the fifth sovereign of the House of Windsor, the dynasty King George V founded in 1917. When Prince Charles comes to the Throne it will mean that for six succes-

sive generations the Crown has passed in an uninterrupted family descent, the first time that this has
occurred since the days of the Early Plantagenets.

In the same month that Prince Charles was born,
the illness of George the Sixth was announced.   He
was suffering, his doctors said, from a severe physical
affliction caused by an obstruction to circulation in
the arteries of the leg.   Prolonged treatment and
complete rest were essential.   He would be unable to
make the tour of Australia and New Zealand that
had been planned for the following Spring.

CHAPTER 8

THE END OF A REIGN

" AND I SAID to the man who stood at the gate of the year : ' Give me a light that I may tread safely into the unknown,' " King George VI had quoted from a poem by Louise Haskins in one of his famous Christmas broadcasts. " And he replied : ' Go out into the darkness and put your hand into the hand of God. That shall be to you better than light and safer than a known way.' "

From that first serious illness of 1948 George the Sixth must have realised that he stood at the gate of the unknown; he was a man, as Mr. Churchill said, who walked with death as his companion. For himself he had no concern. He had " put his hand into the hand of God " and, though he used John Bunyan's words, he spoke for himself when he declared at Christmas 1950, " Whatever comes or does not come I will not be afraid."

Time was getting short. To the nation at large the King's health in those post-war years had become a matter of deep concern; how much graver was the concern of those in the royal family circle, knowing the full facts about His Majesty's condition.

Princess Elizabeth did all that she could to ease the burden of monarchy from her father's shoulders; and the King, though concerned lest she should overtax her strength as he had done his own, concentrated upon the training of his daughter so that, when the day came for her to assume the Crown, she would be as fully equipped for the task as was humanly possible.

Experience flooded upon experience. There was so much to be grasped, so much to be understood, so much of the country and of the Commonwealth to be visited, so many sections of the community to be met. Princess Elizabeth was learning rapidly not only for herself, but for all of her generation. Every new understanding and appreciation, every new experience, whether official or purely personal, she sought to pass on for the practical benefit of others in fulfilment of her pledge of service.

With her parents Princess Elizabeth had toured South Africa. Mainly she had been in the background, although she had named a new dock after herself, and had borne the spotlight of her coming-of-age broadcast. She had travelled eight thousand miles, rushed here and there, ceaselessly on the move. She had discovered that, no matter how comfortable and luxurious the travel, fatigue was unavoidable with so much ground to be covered and so vast a programme to be compressed into so short a time. Though fatigue always follows over-work, it is not a state permissible in royalty. No matter how tired and exhausted, there must always be the appearance of freshness and vitality, of lively interest and sincerity.

The first major tour that King George VI decided his daughter was ready to undertake was the tour of Canada in the autumn of 1951.

When the time came, however, the departure of Princess Elizabeth and the Duke of Edinburgh was delayed by the King's ill-health, which resulted in an operation in September. At last, in an attempt to catch up on an overcrowded programme, the royal couple left by air instead of sea. The operation had been successful, and the King was recovering, but, even so, at such a time no daughter bound by strong ties of love would have chosen voluntarily to travel overseas. To the strain of the tour was therefore added this intimate anxiety which distance and separation helped only to increase. As heiress presumptive, Princess Elizabeth realised, however, that she could not allow her personal feelings to inter-fere with the opportunity to serve Britain and the Commonwealth in a manner not open to anyone else.

The Crown, free of political and financial interests, can inspire the nations of the Commonwealth into unified action : into making the most of their respec-tive resources in the interests of all ; into a realisation that beyond trade and exchange, which in the post-war conditions have been apt to dominate the relationship, lies the true, deeper significance of spiritual brother-hood.

With this understanding of the task before her, Princess Elizabeth left her father's bedside to journey through ten of Canada's provinces. Had she been in a position to criticise the plans made for her, she would probably have commented not upon the amount of work involved, but upon the extent of the tour in the time allotted. The distances to be covered allowed but a fleeting glimpse of the heart of Canada, but fortunately the Canadian people knew that this was a first visit only, and that other tours would follow. Each town, each city on the route, however, meant attendance at civic receptions, and

endless presentations of officials.   Time, in fact, was
taken up by officialdom at the expense of the greater
interest and value in meeting the ordinary people
and obtaining a direct knowledge of their work and
play, their way of life.

In England, Princess Elizabeth had sought to
awaken people to a true understanding of the nation's
various activities, their significance, and the problems
involved.   To attempt to do this in her speeches in
Canada, she appreciated, would be a grave error.
True, the Crown was symbolically as much a part of
Canada as it was of Britain, and in her farewell
broadcast to the people of the Dominion, she drew
attention to the fact.

" I am well aware ", the Princess said, " that the
acclaim you have given us has had a far deeper meaning in it than a personal welcome, and this has often
made me think of the words spoken by the Governor-
General in Ottawa during the first day of our visit.
He said then that the link with the Crown was a
thing of real and tangible strength, and one of the
most important factors in uniting the people of the
Commonwealth into one great brotherhood.   You
have shown me the reality of this, and I thank you
for it.   Destiny has given me the great privilege of
being able to live my life for the service of that
brotherhood.   In these five weeks you have given
me a new strength and inspiration which I know will
always help me in the future.

" We shall take with us memories that will always
draw us back to this country : the towering buildings
of your big cities and the charm of your smaller
communities; the blue skies and golden colours of
autumn—' the fall ' as I have now learned to call

it—and the trees and fields beneath the first snow of winter : all the beauty and the majesty of Canada. I thank you for having shown me these things ; and I am grateful for a glimpse you have given me of the greatness of this nation and the even greater future which is within its grasp.   I have seen this future in the eyes of hundreds and thousands of your children, and have heard it in their voices."

In a farewell speech at Halifax the Duke of Edinburgh echoed his wife's words :

" We take back a fairly comprehensive picture of Canada.   We have seen you at work and at play. We have seen your homes and your children, and we have prayed with you in your churches.   We have seen the forests and the wheat-fields, factories and universities, scientists and armed services, and we have learnt something of your hopes and fears."

Possibly it is mainly upon the symbolism of the Crown that the success of any royal tour in any Commonwealth country depends, and by comparison the holder of the office, the individual, matters little. In Canada, however, on the first major tour abroad in which she was principal, it was Princess Elizabeth herself who captured the hearts in a manner that went far beyond the requirements of formal sovereignty.

It is generally thought that anyone in direct succession to the Throne has a serious outlook and stiff, unbending dignity.   Regal and dignified the Princess was by second nature, but she was also a young woman of grace and charm who could laugh with youthful gaiety when the royal train once accidentally steamed away without her.

On the brief visit to the United States before her return to Britain it was personality alone that won the day. Among countries following a democratic way of life the United States is at the far end of the scale from any form of monarchy. But Princess Elizabeth and her Consort drew cheers of approval from everyone.

The President of the United States was moved to say : " We have had many distinguished visitors here in this city, but never before have we had such a wonderful young couple that so completely captured the hearts of us all."

In his address Mr. Truman continued : " This country is built upon principles that we have inherited from the British people—our love of liberty, our system of justice, which is based upon the English Common Law, our language—these and many other things have given us a strong feeling of kinship.

" Over the years we have built these ties into a remarkable international friendship. We have had our differences in the past, but today it would be just as hard to imagine a war between our countries as it would be to imagine another war between the States of this country. It just could not happen.

" I hope the day will come soon when the same thing will be true among all nations of the world—when war will be impossible in the world. That depends in great measure upon how well our two countries stick together and work for world peace. I am sure we will do a better job for world peace because your visit has tightened the bonds between us."

From Canada, Princess Elizabeth returned with " a new sense of faith in the progress of mankind.

" For none of the doubts or difficulties that face us in Europe are going to hold back the Canadians," she said. " They are going to ensure for themselves the survival of all those things for which we have fought in this country through the ages, and which we treasure—justice, liberty, opportunity for all, and kindliness between men and men. And by so doing they are going to ensure this for others, too."

At Guildhall, in London, the Prime Minister welcomed back the heiress presumptive with the nation's thanks to her " for what you have done for us, and to Providence for having endowed you with the gifts and personality which are not only precious to the British Commonwealth and Empire and its islands at home, but will play their part in assuring the forward march of human society all the world over ".

At Sandringham King George's mother, Queen Mary, his wife and daughters and grandchildren, his brother and sisters-in-law, his nephews and nieces of Kent and Gloucester, gathered about him to make Christmas 1951 one of the most complete and memorable family occasions. Though he was still convalescent and his doctors were anxious that he should be spared even the slightest strain, in the intimacy of his own private circle he could not forget, at that greatest of family festivals, the wider family of which he was head : the peoples of whom he thought as " one great family, for that is how we are learning to live. We all belong to each other. We all need each other. It is in serving each other and in sacrificing for our own common good that we are finding our true life."

Although far from well, King George VI made up his mind to broadcast at Christmas as usual. He

wanted to join his peoples at their own celebrations in
their own homes to give them his personal greetings.
He agreed with his doctors to record his message
beforehand, so that the strain on his voice and strength
might be eased as much as possible.

Courage, however, could not hide from his voice
the fact that he was still a sick man as he thanked his
doctors and nurses for their care and devotion, and
his peoples for their solicitude over his health.   He
spoke of friendliness and kindness; of how precious
this spirit was in an age often hard and cruel, and
needing the " example of tolerance and understanding
that runs like a golden thread through the great and
diverse family of the British Commonwealth of
Nations ".

" I think," said King George VI in his last message
to his peoples, " that among all the blessings which
we may count today, the chief one is that we are a
friendly people."

Once again his tour of Australia and New Zealand,
which had had to be cancelled in 1949 and had been
planned afresh for 1952, was out of the question.   The
doctors advised that he must continue to rest until
he had sufficiently recovered his strength to reap the
full benefit of a sea cruise in H.M.S. *Vanguard*.

Instead, therefore, it was arranged that Princess
Elizabeth, with the Duke of Edinburgh, should
undertake the Australasian tour in the place of her
father.   From London Airport on a bitter wintry
day the King waved farewell to his daughter as she left
by air to enjoy a few days' holiday in Kenya that
would refresh her for the royal tour ahead.   Standing
within six feet of his Majesty, I remember the long,
searching look which he gave his daughter as she

turned to wave for the last time from the door of the aircraft. He was never to see her again.

George the Sixth returned to Sandringham, where he was as free as he ever could be from the trappings of monarchy and state; where the villagers neither stared nor intruded, but accepted him naturally as their squire.

That week-end the weather was still cold, but fine. By the frozen lake the King watched his grandson, Prince Charles, learning to skate.

On Tuesday, February 5, 1952, free from pain and in good spirits, the King went shooting. After a quiet family dinner-party he took a last walk round the grounds of the house where he was born, the home that he loved best of all; the grounds to which his mother, Queen Mary, had devoted such a labour of love in their re-planning and creation into a scene of joy and beauty. As he walked in the still calm of the winter evening he was already looking forward to a shoot the following day if the weather held.

The King was surely a man content and at peace. There is no stage at which training for sovereignty can be said to end, but the manner in which his daughter had fulfilled her first major rôle in that mission to Canada must have exceeded even a proud father's expectations and given him the assurance that when the time came for her to wear the Crown she would not falter. He had seen her happily married, and knew that she would have the love and support of her devoted husband and family to help her to bear the burden. He had seen, too, the affection and esteem that she had earned in the hearts of the people.

George the Sixth, by the Grace of God, of Great Britain, Northern Ireland, and the British Dominions beyond the Seas, King, Defender of the Faith, retired peacefully to his room and fell asleep for the last time.

In Kenya, his twenty-five-year-old daughter was making her way along a jungle path to a " hide " from which she could watch the big game. Suddenly from out of the shadows an elephant emerged and stood in her path. Without flinching, Princess Elizabeth continued to walk steadily towards the elephant until she had reached the " hide ". Quietly she climbed the ladder to the platform built among the branches of the tree.

" Ma'am," said Mr. Sherborne Walker, the owner of the Treetops Hotel, " if you have the same courage in facing whatever the future sends you, as you have in facing an elephant at ten yards, we are going to be very fortunate."

CHAPTER 9

ELIZABETH IS QUEEN

THE fact that the new Queen Elizabeth was abroad at the time of her accession created no problems. Edward I was proclaimed King during his absence in Palestine on the Crusades, and his coronation did not take place until two years afterwards. The last sovereign to succeed to the throne while abroad was George I, whose journey back to Britain took him nearly two months. In 1952 Queen Elizabeth spanned half the world by air to reach the capital of her realm in less than twenty hours.

While the Queen was beginning the first stage of her four-thousand-miles flight home, the Accession Council met at the Ambassador's Court of St. James' Palace for the formal proclamation of her accession, and Members of Parliament and peers began to take the Oath of Allegiance to their new sovereign.

The Accession Council is a much older body than the Privy Council, which was originally an assembly entrusted with the King's secret business. Older than the House of Lords and going back beyond the Great Council of the Realm, the council of mediaeval kings, the Accession Council probably has its origin in the Anglo-Saxon Witenagemot, the assembly which met to choose and proclaim a new sovereign. Numbering over three hundred members, the Accession Council includes, in addition to the members of the late sovereign's Privy Council, the "Lords Spiritual and Temporal of this realm" and "numbers of other principal gentlemen of quality, with the Lord Mayor, Aldermen, and Citizens of London".

The proclamation was, of course, no more than a traditional formality, as was the subsequent Accession Declaration to uphold the Protestant Succession to the Throne and to maintain the security of the Established Church of Scotland. The heiress presumptive had automatically become Queen the instant her father died, and her accession was in no way dependent upon these ceremonies.

Up to the thirteenth century there was invariably an "interregnum"—a period between the death of one king and the crowning of his successor—when the country was without sovereign or formal rule. Justice has always been—and still is—a part of the royal prerogative, which meant that while there was no sovereign there was also no "Fountain of Justice". The King's Peace temporarily ceased to exist, and crime could be committed without fear of punishment.

"There was tribulation soon in the land, for every man that could forthwith robbed another," recorded an observer at the time of the death of Henry I.

When Henry III died, the absence of his heir, Edward I, with the Crusades meant a long "interregnum" before he could return to be crowned, and this would have resulted in an impossible situation. The King's Peace was therefore sworn forthwith, and on the day that his father was buried it was proclaimed that the reign of Edward I had begun.

By the time of Edward IV the rule was established that upon the death of a sovereign no "interregnum",

This photograph of Princess Elizabeth was taken shortly before her visit to Canada in 1951.

or break in formal rule, occurred.   The Crown thus became a symbol of power and authority that continued without regard for the death of a sovereign : it passed automatically without interruption to the heir.   In 1608 it was legally upheld that by the laws of England there was no such thing as a state of " interregnum ", and that " coronation is but a royal ornament and solemnisation of the royal descent, but no part of the title ".

Thus, while Queen Elizabeth the Second was still on her way back to England, Parliament, Privy Council, Justice, and all Crown appointments continued uninterrupted without the necessity of any action on her part.   His Majesty's Forces had immediately become Her Majesty's Forces; King's Counsel had automatically changed to Queen's Counsel.

On February 8, 1952, Queen Elizabeth held the first meeting of her Privy Council at St. James' Palace.

" By the sudden death of my dear father I am called to assume the duties and responsibility of sovereignty," she said in her Accession Speech to the Council.

" At this time of deep sorrow it is a profound consolation to me to be assured of the sympathy which you and all my peoples feel toward me, to my mother and my sister, and to the other members of my family.   My father was our revered and beloved head, as he was of the wider family of his subjects.   The grief which his loss brings is shared among us all.

" My heart is too full for me to say more to you to-day than that I shall always work, as my father did throughout his reign, to uphold constitutional govern-

Above :   *Princess Elizabeth and the Duke of Edinburgh with their children, Prince Charles and Princess Anne.*

Below :   *Buckingham Palace, the Royal Family's home in London.*

ment and to advance the happiness and prosperity of my peoples, spread as they are all the world over. I know that in my resolve to follow his shining example of service and devotion I shall be inspired by the loyalty and affection of those whose Queen I have been called to be, and by the counsel of their elected Parliaments.

" I pray that God will help me to discharge worthily this heavy task that has been laid upon me so early in my life."

Shortly afterwards, at 11 a.m., resplendent in cockaded hats and brilliant, gold-emblazoned tabards, the Kings-of-Arms, the Heralds and the Pursuivants gathered on the balcony at St. James' Palace. Preceded by a fanfare from the State trumpeters, Sir George Bellew, Garter King of Arms, unrolled a scroll of parchment and read the first of the series of public proclamations that would echo through the cities of Great Britain, Northern Ireland, and the Commonwealth :

" Whereas it hath pleased Almighty God to call to His Mercy our late Sovereign Lord King *George* the Sixth of Blessed and Glorious Memory by whose Decease the Crown is solely and rightfully come to the High and Mighty Princess *Elizabeth Alexandra Mary* : We, therefore, the Lords Spiritual and Temporal of this Realm, being here assisted with these of His late Majesty's Privy Council, with representatives of other members of the Commonwealth, with other Principal Gentlemen of Quality, with the Lord Mayor, Aldermen and Citizens of London, do now hereby with one voice and Consent of Tongue and Heart publish and proclaim that the High and Mighty Princess *Elizabeth Alexandra Mary* is now, by the Death of our late Sovereign of Happy Memory, become Queen *Elizabeth* the Second, by the Grace of God Queen of this Realm and of all Her other Realms and Territories, Head of the Commonwealth, Defender of the Faith, to whom Her lieges do acknowledge all Faith and constant Obedience, with hearty and humble Affection; beseeching God, by whom Kings and Queens do reign, to bless the Royal Princess *Elizabeth* the Second with long and happy Years to reign over us.

"God Save The Queen."

Queen Elizabeth was the first sovereign to be proclaimed "Head of the Commonwealth", a title which was the result of India's decision to become a republic although still remaining a member of the Commonwealth of Nations, and which replaced her great-great-grandmother's title of Empress of India.

There was another notable alteration of the terms in which her father's accession had been proclaimed. He had been described as "Of Great Britain, Ireland, and the British Dominions beyond the Seas". Queen Elizabeth was referred to as "Queen of this Realm and all her other realms and territories".

In the House of Commons Mr. Churchill gave the following explanation :

"The House will observe in the Royal Proclamation the importance and significance of the word 'realm'. There was a time, not so long ago, when the word 'dominion' was greatly esteemed, but now the many nations and races have found in the word 'realm' an expression of their sense of unity, combined in most cases with positive allegiance to the Crown or proud and respectful association with it. Thus we go forward on our long and anxious journey, moving together in freedom and in hope, spread across the oceans and under the sky and climate though we be."

Some responsible sources believed that the change had resulted from representation from one or more of the Dominions. Canada, in particular, had on one or two occasions given evidence of a desire to change from the status of a self-governing Dominion to that of a sister Kingdom of Great Britain with the title, " Kingdom of Canada ". There was more support for this belief when Canada proclaimed Queen Elizabeth's accession with the words " our own lawful and rightful liege Lady Elizabeth II by the Grace of God, of Great Britain, Ireland, and the British Dominions beyond the Seas, Queen. Defender of the Faith, supreme Liege Lady in and over Canada." South Africa, using the same original description that had applied to her father, added the words " Supreme Sovereign in and over South Africa ", while Australia followed the same form as Canada.

The flags and standards that had temporarily soared to the mastheads for the proclamation of the accession of the Queen, returned to the half-mast position as the nation mourned the passing of a beloved sovereign.

From the small village church at Sandringham, where he had been guarded by gamekeepers from his estate, the dead King was brought to Westminster Hall to lie in State, while night and day an endless train of his people filed past in silent homage. As I watched one night that moving panorama of tribute and love I broadcast these impressions :

It is dark in New Palace Yard at Westminster tonight. As I look down from this old, leaded window I can see the ancient courtyard dappled

with little pools of light where the lamps of
London try to pierce the biting, wintry gloom—
and fail. Moving through the darkness of the
night is an even darker stream of human beings,
coming, almost noiselessly, from under a long,
white canopy that crosses the pavement and ends
at the great doors of Westminster Hall.   They
speak very little, these people, but their footsteps
sound faintly as they cross the yard and go out
through the gates, back into the night from
which they came.

They are passing in their thousands through
the hall of history while history is being made.
No one knows from where they come or where
they go, but they are the people, and to watch
them pass is to see the nation pass.

It is very simple, this Lying-in-State of a dead
King, and of incomparable beauty.   High above,
all light and shadow and rich in carving, is the
massive roof that Richard the Second put over
the great hall.   From the roof the light slants
down in clear, straight beams, unclouded by
any dust, and gathers in a pool at one place.
There lies the coffin of the King.

The oak of Sandringham is hidden beneath the
rich golden folds of the Standard.   The slow
flicker of the candles touches gently the gems of
the Imperial Crown, even the ruby that King
Henry wore at Agincourt.   It touches the deep
purple of the velvet cushion and the cool white
flowers of the only wreath that lies upon the
flag.   How moving can such simplicity be !
How real the tears of those who pass and see it,
and come out again, as they do at this moment, in

unbroken stream, to the cold, dark night and a little privacy for their thoughts!

Who can know what they are thinking? Does that blind man whom they lead so carefully down the thick carpet, sense around him the presence of history? Does he know that Kings and Queens have feasted here and stood their trial and gone to death? And that little woman with an airman by her side—does she feel the ghosts that must be here in the shadows of the hall? The men and the women of those tumultuous days of long ago, of Chaucer, Essex, Anne Boleyn, Charles and Cromwell, Warren Hastings, and those early Georges? Or does she, and do all those other seventy thousand of the nation who will have passed through this day alone, think only of the sixth George : the faithful George who lies there now, guarded by the living statues of his officers and Gentlemen at Arms and Yeomen of the Guard? For in the few seconds that are all that can be given to each subject to pass by his dead King, there is colour and splendour and loveliness beyond compare.

Never safer, better guarded, lay a sleeping King than this, with a golden light to warm his resting-place and the muffled tread of his devoted people to keep him company. They come from a mile away in the night, moving pace by pace for hours of waiting, come into the silent majesty of the scene and, as silently, leave again.

Two hundred thousand may come to Westminster this week, but for every one of them there will be a thousand scattered about the world who cannot come, but who may be here in their thoughts at this moment. They will know that the sorrow of one man, one woman, or one child that passes by the King in London is their sorrow too.

For how true tonight of George the Faithful is that single sentence spoken by an unknown man of his beloved father : " The sunset of his death tinged the whole world's sky."

PART III

MANTLE OF MONARCHY

CHAPTER 10

THE STORY OF KINGSHIP

HISTORICALLY, Queen Elizabeth the Second is the fourth sovereign of the House of Windsor, and the fortieth since the Norman Conquest. She is the twelfth sovereign of Great Britain as legally constituted by the Act of Union between England and Scotland in 1707, although the Scots King James VI had adopted the title King of Great Britain a hundred years before, when he became James I of England. James, in fact, wore two crowns. He was King of England and King of Scots. He had of course been crowned as such in Scotland before he ever came to England, but his successors, Charles I and Charles II, were also crowned in Scotland as well as in England. It was not until the Act of Union that the two Crowns united in one Crown of Great Britain, just as the Scots Parliament merged into Westminster.

To her peoples at large, however, the question of style of title was less important than the human side of the Crown, the personality of the Queen. What mattered in the eyes of her subjects was the fact that Queen Elizabeth the Second was, as Mr. Churchill summed up, a fair and youthful figure, princess, wife, and mother, the " heir to all our traditions and glories, never greater than in her father's day, and to all our perplexities and dangers, never greater in peacetime than now. She is also heir to our united strength and loyalty."

In the last inheritance of united strength and loyalty lies the promise of the new reign. Though the world is sorely vexed and troubled, the Crown has never gleamed more brightly. No sovereign has ascended a throne more securely based and with such inspiring assurance from the knowledge of the place she has already won in the hearts of her peoples.

The historian, J. R. Green, wrote of the first Elizabeth's accession : " Never had the fortunes of England sunk to a lower ebb than at the moment when Elizabeth mounted the Throne. . . . England's one hope lay in the character of her Queen."

Once again the fortunes of England are low. But in the character of the Queen how much greater is the advantage with which the second Elizabethan age begins. Her character is well known to all; it is the product of a happy childhood, based on the highest Christian principles, and secure in the knowledge of family love and unity.

The strength of the British monarchy and the British Constitution lies in the unwritten law. Throughout the centuries the principle and practice of the Constitution and the Crown's place in the Constitution have developed sometimes by accident, sometimes by intent. Part of the Constitution is defined in statutes, part can be found in decisions at law; much of it depends entirely upon tradition, custom, and practice.

The terms of the British Constitution have never been written out in one legal document as is the case, for instance, in the United States.   There the American Constitution was framed by Benjamin Franklin and his associates in 1788 as the basis of the federal government of the United States and the text, with amendments, is used by the Supreme Court for deciding whether legislation is constitutional or not.

Nor has there been any attempt, as there was in France, to qualify to the letter the powers and authority of the Crown.   Here again some of the Crown's powers have been defined by statutes, but in the true sense the royal prerogative is vested in the common law, the unwritten law of the realm.   The word "prerogative" means the rights of the sovereign, who is theoretically subject to no restriction. Today the prerogative is generally accepted as embracing all the powers and privileges that the Crown derives from ancient usage and from the custom of the nation.

The nearest attempt at laying down an English Constitution was the Instrument of Government drawn up and put into force by Cromwell and his Army during the Commonwealth.   This, however, was withdrawn after the Restoration, and has had no lasting influence upon the Constitution, which continues as always to develop in its own way, building and modelling upon the past, modifying and adding to the old.   In 1872 Professor E. A. Freeman wrote of the growth of the English Constitution :

" The continued national life of the people, notwithstanding foreign conquests and internal revolutions, has remained unbroken for fourteen hundred years.   At no moment has the tie between the present and the past been wholly rent asunder; at no moment have Englishmen sat down to put together a wholly new Constitution, in obedience to some dazzling theory. Each step in our growth has been the natural consequence of some earlier step; each change in our Law and Constitution has been, not the bringing in of anything wholly new, but the development and improvement of something that was already old.''

The passage is as true today as it was in Queen Victoria's time. The Constitution is as much a living thing as the nation that it serves, having the same regular growth and expansion. With no rigid pattern to be followed the Crown has never become a hardened mould presenting to any generation the same clear-cut ideas on a '' take-it-or-leave-it '' basis. The individual sovereign has been able to bring his own interpretation of the influence of the Crown in the affairs of the nation, and upon the sovereign's personal discretion has rested the popularity and even the continued existence of the Throne. The result is that, throughout the centuries, the Crown has gradually changed from owning the people to belonging to them.

It is, of course, unconstitutional for the Queen to act at all except through or with the advice of her ministers, and consequently with the will of the people. From the earliest days, the Sovereign has needed the agreement and assistance of his subjects to put his powers effectively into operation. He began by calling together his most powerful barons into a council to help him in money matters, in providing an army, and in civil administration. Later, the smaller landowners, and then the burgesses, representatives of the chartered boroughs, were added to the Council.

Simon de Montfort is often credited with being the founder of the House of Commons because in 1265 he summoned a national assembly of knights from certain towns and shires, and a large number of clergy to discuss the question of money supplies for the king. The birth of Parliament as we know it today really began thirty years later, however, when Edward I established the Model Parliament of " those who pray, those who fight, those who work " —the clergy, the barons, and the commons, the three estates of the realm. At last representatives of organised communities of shires and towns—" les communes " from which the House of Commons derives its name—were meeting regularly to approve taxation to meet the expenses of State, and to add their own support to the statutes of the King.

When Henry IV of Lancaster deposed Richard II he announced that he would rule by " common advice, counsel and consent " of " honourable, wise, and discreet persons of his kingdom ", and his reign drew the comment : " Never before and never again for more than two hundred years were the Commons so strong as they were under Henry IV."

The consent of subject as a means of government may have taken two hundred years to develop into practice, but the principle was established not only as an occasional custom, but also as a legal opinion.

Sir John Fortescue, a former Chief Justice of England, described the position between sovereign and subject in this way : " He [the King] can neither make any alteration or change in the laws of the realm without the consent of his subjects, nor burden them against their wills with strange impositions." In practice, the royal prerogative now protects the rights of the people and ensures that their will prevails.

To understand the position that Queen Elizabeth occupies today in the life of this and " all her other realms " let me turn back for a moment the pages of history.

The origin of kingship is lost in the dim mists of the past. Two early cavemen, perhaps, were engaged in a struggle to the death when a third man helped them to settle their dispute. The fame of this man's wisdom passed from mouth to mouth. Others began to bring him their problems and seek his advice. The status of a wise man, a leader, had come into being. Men began to look outside their own family circles and acknowledged the leadership of one man, a chief under whom families became united into a tribe.

Through war, both as a result of conquest and also by joining together to resist attack, there grew a sense of racial and national unity, and the power and influence of the chief, the king, increased correspondingly. Kinship was extending to kingship. Like the early tribal chieftains who were chiefs of tribes, not territories, so the first kings in our history were kings of people, and not domains. Egbert, for instance, who began his reign in A.D. 827, claimed to be the first " King of the English ".

Even in those days the king acted only with his advisers—in Anglo-Saxon times the Great Council known as the Witan. This consisted of various officials, nobles, bishops, and king's thegns. The Saxon king had absolute powers, but the use of them was checked because he had to act through or with the Witan. Apart from this, as well, the king did not wish to offend the customs of his race.

The Witan, in electing the king, confined their choice to members of the royal family, which was considered to be descended from gods. Though the field of choice was so limited, the election of the king and the practice of consultation with the Witan combined to make the king to some extent representative of his peoples : he was responsible for justice, law and order, the preservation of peace, and their protection in time of war. Nothing so unites a nation as threat of invasion, and the attacks by the Danes did much to increase the powers of the Throne. Finally, Canute's defeat of Edmund Ironside caused the Witan to go beyond the range of royal birth and elect Canute as their King.

This change in custom caused so much strife and quarrelling over Canute's successors that Saxon monarchy was saved only by the Norman Conquest. Even William the Conqueror, although he had won his crown by force, was loud in his proclamation that it was his rightful inheritance, a claim which was without any foundation. The theory of heredity—the passing from father to son—as the most convenient method of ensuring a stable and peaceable succession was already taking shape.

Both the hereditary principle and the Crown itself were vastly strengthened by William's introduction of the feudal system. This provided him not only with a self-supporting administration, but also with a trained army scattered throughout the country and ready for immediate action in the event of emergency. It was on much the same lines as the twentieth-century's Territorial Force. Under the feudal system all land was held on lease from the Crown in return for the supply each year of a certain number of warriors for so many days' service. This made the barons entirely dependent upon the Crown, whose hold upon the loyalty and service of every great landowner was strengthened by personal relationship and individual contract.

The landowners who held their land direct from the king as tenants-in-chief could in turn sub-let it, but William took the precaution of requiring that every vassal, no matter from whom he held his land, should owe above his duties to his immediate lord a prime allegiance and military service direct to the Crown. All vassals thus became king's men, and this removed the threat that they might one day be mobilised by their barons against the Crown.

The feudal system of inheritance also helped to secure the power of the Crown. By establishing as sole legal heir the eldest son, who, like his father, would continue to hold the land on a military tenure, the Crown's hold over the country continued undiminished. Further, if a tenant-in-chief had no heir, the property passed into the Crown's personal possession. This automatic inheritance of property, together with other acquisitions by confiscation for misdemeanours, made the sovereign increasingly powerful, and consequently, on his death, his eldest son, to whom the property passed intact under the same system of inheritance that applied to everyone else. By reason of the power which the eldest son of the king accordingly inherited, the elective character of the succession to the Throne began to give place to the principle of hereditary right.

The change was a gradual process, and for four centuries the succession varied between those whose claims lay in descent and those who occupied the throne by " election " as a process which developed into title by Act of Parliament. Generally the success of the claim to the throne depended also upon a strong arm, but by 1216 the hereditary principle was sufficiently recognised to allow the accession of the nine-year-old Henry III. Whether a sovereign wore the Crown by parliamentary title or through direct inheritance, he generally took pains to establish himself as king according to both view-points on the monarchy. If the throne came to him by descent he passed an Act of Parliament to confirm his title. If he were elected to the throne he was just as eager to establish his hereditary claim as well.

Not until the times of Henry VII and his son, Henry VIII, was the law of hereditary succession at last established in practice. When Henry VIII was crowned it was the first time in a hundred years that the succession to the Throne had not been disputed. With the subsequent exception of the case of James Stuart, hereditary monarchy had come to stay.

In recent times, the British system of a limited hereditary monarchy has made possible the steadfast continuation of the Constitution and the national way of life amid all the inconstancy and turbulence of the present century.

As for the luxury of the position bestowed by accident of birth, the first Queen Elizabeth, who ruled where Queen Elizabeth the Second now reigns,

*H.M. the Queen drives in State from Bucking-
ham Palace to open the first Parliament of
her reign.*

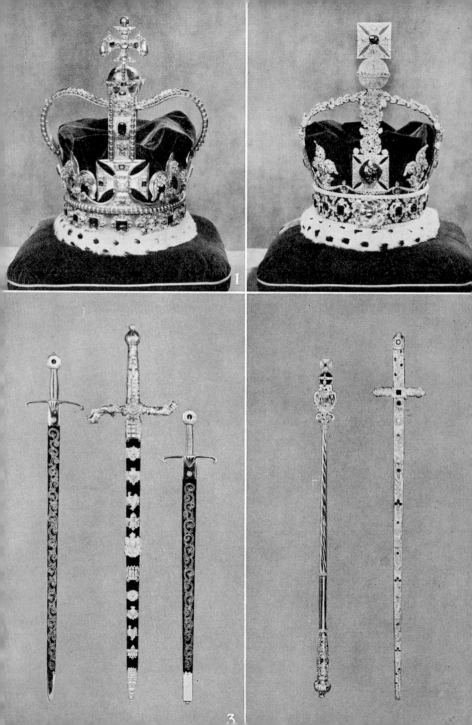

said in November 1601, after forty-two years on the throne :

" To be a King and wear a crown is a thing more glorious to them that see than it is pleasant to them that bear it."

THE STATE REGALIA :

(1) *ST. EDWARD'S CROWN is the Crown of England. It is used only at the coronation of a sovereign.*

(2) *THE IMPERIAL STATE CROWN is worn by the reigning monarch on all State occasions after coronation.*

(3) *THE THREE SWORDS OF STATE.*

(4) *THE ROYAL SCEPTRE and the JEWELLED SWORD.*

CHAPTER II

THE CROWN TODAY

THE Stuarts claimed that the king could do no wrong because he acted in accordance with divine will; but the principle that the sovereign can do no wrong applies equally to Queen Elizabeth today, although for different reasons.

Her powers as Sovereign are exercised not by herself personally, but through the ministers who bear sole responsibility for all actions taken in the Queen's name. The law does not acknowledge any circumstances in which the sovereign might commit or institute an unlawful act, and servants of the Crown may not plead in excuse for a misdemeanour that it was committed by royal command. Instead of giving the sovereign complete freedom, the transfer of personal responsibility from sovereign to official has the opposite effect. An official who knows that he will bear the full consequence of the Crown's action is naturally going to resist any attempt upon the part of the sovereign to commit any deed of doubtful legality.

Queen Anne, always concerned that no one should be mistaken into thinking that she was to be frightened into agreement because she was a woman, was the last sovereign to attend debates in the House of Lords, and she had no scruples about using her presence to influence policy. She was also the last sovereign to make use of the veto. The power of veto still lies with our Queen Elizabeth, but she could execute it constitutionally only upon the advice of her ministers. As all Bills brought before the Queen are those introduced and passed by her ministers, they are hardly likely to advise her to veto their own measures, and it is most improbable that the Norman French phrase, " *Le Roy s'avisera* ", by which the Royal Assent is withheld, will be heard in the present reign.

George I of Hanover, who followed Anne to the throne, understood practically no English. Unable to follow what was taking place at the meetings of his ministers, he decided to stay away, and started a custom that has since been followed. His absence brought the need for a minister to preside in his place —a Prime Minister—and, without in any way interfering with the prerogative of the Crown, gave also further evidence of the sovereign's freedom from responsibility for the acts in his name.

Hitherto the king had possessed a definite say in the government of his realm, ruling in fact through his ministers. Now, by the accident of a German king who knew no English, the tables began to turn, and it became the ministers who governed through the instrument of the Crown. This is the basis of our present-day constitutional monarchy.

The recent Crown Proceedings Act of 1947 has brought a notable change in the application of the law that the king can do no wrong. Until the operation of this Act, ministers in their rôle of agents of the Crown enjoyed the same immunity from legal proceedings as the sovereign.

As a result of this new Act proceedings can now be brought against the Crown in the shape of the appropriate minister or government department, or, alternatively, the Attorney-General. Today the maxim that the sovereign can do no wrong applies only to the person of Queen Elizabeth herself.

It is the Queen's prerogative to declare war and make peace. It is she who negotiates treaties, receives foreign diplomats, and generally maintains international relations. The Queen also appoints the leading officers of Church and State.

One prime advantage that the prerogative possesses over the statutory powers of the Crown is the fact that there is no necessity for Parliament to be consulted in advance about the use of the prerogative. This privilege is of particular value in matters relating to the armed forces, foreign affairs, honours, and appointments, which are not always suitable for discussion in the House.

The royal prerogative is normally exercised upon the advice of the ministers, but it is generally agreed that there are two cases in which the Queen can exercise her prerogative without the advice, or even against the advice, of her ministers. These are the selection of a prime minister where the leadership of a party returned to power is not definitely established, and the dissolution of parliament.

The royal prerogative is an important part of the Constitution. To preserve that Constitution is Queen Elizabeth's first responsibility, and it is for this purpose that the authority of the prerogative remains vested in her. In practice, of course, the prerogative is no longer a sovereign's privilege. It has become instead the privilege of the people, and the Queen is there to see that their rights are protected and that their will prevails. When it is not possible to ascertain the people's wishes directly upon any matter, then the Queen is constitutionally bound to give her wholehearted support and confidence to the party in power, the Government of the day. That is the only opinion allowed her.

The Queen executes her formal acts of government in three ways : by Orders in Council, by Warrants, Commissions, and Orders under the Sign Manual, and by Proclamations, Writs, Letters Patent, Charters, and other documents under the Great Seal of the Realm.

An Order in Council is a resolution passed by a meeting of her Privy Council, and may concern a matter coming within either her prerogative or statutory powers. By Orders in Council, too, the Queen regulates the discipline and administration of the Crown departments.

Under the Sign Manual the Queen signs with her own hand documents relating to appointments, instructions to governors of colonies, and also issues pardons. These warrants signed by the Queen are countersigned by the appropriate minister, who accepts the responsibility for the act. It was under a Sign Manual warrant that Queen Victoria exercised her prerogative to abolish the purchase of commissions in the Army.

It is under the Great Seal, first used by Edward the Confessor and now kept in the custody of the Lord Chancellor, that the Queen issues proclamations of a state of war or emergency, or the dissolution of parliament. No one but the Queen under the Great Seal may issue proclamations, and these are restricted to acts of the prerogative or to calling attention to the statutory law. Once a Proclamation is published in the *London Gazette* it is valid in law as an Act of Parliament.

Under the Great Seal the Queen signs treaties with other nations and causes writs for parliamentary elections to be issued. By Letters Patent under the Great Seal titles are conferred, Royal Commissions are appointed, new offices are constituted, and provision is made for the government of colonies. It was by Letters Patent under the Great Seal that King George VI decreed that the children of the marriage between Princess Elizabeth and the Duke of Edinburgh should " at all time hold and enjoy the style, title or attribute of Royal Highness and the titular dignity of Prince or Princess ".

Often the ways in which the Queen's Pleasure may be expressed are interwoven. Thus parliament is dissolved by Proclamation, and an Order in Council commands the issue of the writs for the summoning of a new parliament ; and apart from a few statutory exceptions, a Sign Manual Warrant is necessary to authorise the use of the Great Seal.

There are many other incidental rights appertaining to the Queen. She decides what the Royal Arms shall be, and grants licences for their use. She approves the occasions on which salutes shall be fired and the number of guns that shall be used. All treasure trove belongs to the Queen ; so do any whales or sturgeon caught within territorial waters and any white swans, provided they are wild and unmarked.

The Queen is the owner of the foreshore—the land between the high-water and low-water marks—and also of the sea-bed in all territorial waters throughout the Dominions. Hers is the sole right of printing, or granting licences to print, the Bible and Book of Common Prayer, and State documents. The building and supervision of harbours, the grant of markets and fisheries, the award of civil list pensions, the coinage, all come with the royal prerogative. Royal tours, receptions, formal meetings of the Council, the holding of investitures, the signing of an endless succession of State documents, the granting of audiences, the patronage of art, music, drama, literature, science, sport, charity, welfare, and almost every form of national activity—these are but some of the regular routine duties of the Queen.

The royal palaces, which belong to the nation and are the Queen's by tenure of the Crown only, are free of rates and taxes, but these are paid in full on her personal property, such as the Sandringham estate. If she were to fail to pay, however, there would be no means of recovery, as the Queen cannot be sued in her own courts. Though she may hold and buy private property, she is not permitted to rent from a subject. Nor is she able to vote.

Greatest disability of all, however, that the wearing of the Crown brings to Queen Elizabeth is the isolation from normal everyday life. Queen Victoria once complained that she did not know what a railway ticket looked like. Careful preparation and training for the Throne, with a remarkable freedom to mix with those who are now her subjects, have given Queen Elizabeth an awareness and understanding that will humanise the aloofness thrust upon her with the Crown.

The position of the husband of a Queen Regnant, however, is not prescribed in the British Constitution.

He is simply a subject with no special privileges over any other subject, and it is thus in the rôle of intermediary between the Queen and her people that the Duke of Edinburgh is able to render unique and valuable service. From the Duke, Queen Elizabeth can obtain the ungilded truth about national affairs and the real views of the people. With the Duke, Her Majesty can discuss the problems of monarchy with a freedom and intimacy impossible in audiences with her ministers, however privileged.

It is said that the burden of monarchy falls doubly upon a Queen Regnant, who has to undertake not only the complete duties of a King but also those of a Queen Consort, which are so feminine in character that they cannot be passed to her husband. The Duke of Edinburgh, however, has already fashioned his own rôle in relation to the Crown by relieving his wife of some of those duties his position and sex enable him to carry out more thoroughly than the Queen could hope to do.

Within the first weeks of the new reign he had made a personal investigation of Britain's industry and scientific research, visiting collieries, heavy industries, the National Physical Laboratory, and Harwell. They were visits that went far beyond the formal reception committees and presentation of executives. In a manner denied to the Queen, he was able to piece together a comprehensive survey of the heart of British industry.

Albert, Queen Victoria's Prince Consort, sought to encourage industry from the top by inspiring the directors and manufacturers themselves. Philip, the Duke of Edinburgh, has chosen to tackle the job from the bottom.   It was the men themselves that he talked to about their work and their problems, and he had no hesitation about going down the pits and watching the miners at work at the coal-face. In addition to the understanding that he was acquiring for himself, for the Queen, for the nation, his visits themselves proved valuable incentives to morale and production.

The Duke of Edinburgh subsequently summed up his impressions of his tours in a speech to the University of Wales, in which he named the forces of prosperity as science, craftsmanship, and labour, the knowledge, the ability, and the will to work.

" First," he said, " I found there is a great wealth of scientific and technological knowledge ready to be used. Part of this store has been used with great success but, by and large, there is still a widespread disregard on the part of industry towards the use of scientific knowledge.

" Secondly, I learned that the quality of work and enthusiasm of working-people depends almost entirely on human relations.

" Thirdly, I am completely convinced that those who say that craftsmanship is dead are quite wrong. Given the tools, and it is the tools that have changed and not the men, British craftsmen are as far ahead as ever."

Constitutionally, Queen Elizabeth cannot reject or oppose the advice of her ministers. If, however, she thinks the advice unsound she is entitled to express her opinion by warning them that it might be better not to follow the line of action proposed. The notion of professional statesmen, who have reached their position by long years of experience, consulting and being warned by a sovereign who owes his or her position entirely to accident of birth is not as strange as it may seem.

Governments change and ministers go out of power : the sovereign remains always at the head of the nation, gaining an increasing practical experience on a wide and varied scale such as not even a prime minister enjoys. Quite obviously no one can remain continually consulted and advised by the foremost brains in the country without gaining a wide experience and a wisdom and opinion of practical value to the interests of the nation. At present the direct influence of Queen Elizabeth springs primarily from her youth, from her energy and enthusiasm, which give an impetus to the wisdom and prudence of her elder statesmen; but as the years pass and other ministers appear on the scene, Queen Elizabeth will know how their predecessors and how the opposition ministries tackled the problems of state.

The same advantage of youthful accession was shared by Queen Victoria and Elizabeth I, who, with Queen Anne, have given birth to the belief that Britain always prospers with a woman on the throne. These were reigns of greatness indeed, but not one of those queens had greatness thrust upon her. It had to be earned.

There is no doubt that a woman on the throne brings out the chivalry in man and fires him with a more adventurous spirit and to greater achievement. In the words of General Gordon, " England was made by adventurers, not by its Government, and I believe it will only hold its place by adventurers."

This was the case with the first Elizabeth, inspiring men like Drake, Raleigh, Frobisher, and Hawkins to explore the unknown for the honour of the Queen. It is already so in the reign of the second Elizabeth, in which men like the late John Derry and Neville Duke have achieved so much in the dimensions of space and sound.

Every age has had its share of discoveries and developments. The inventions of bygone times— which we now take for granted—were just as amazing to people then as atomic energy and space exploration are to the present generation. Each age has ventured into an unknown fraught with the same sense of uncertainty, risk, and adventure. Throughout them all the Crown has remained steadfast, guided by those same basic principles that have applied equally to the national characteristics and way of life, whether arrow, cannon-ball, or atom-bomb has been the latest weapon, whether the Englishman's castle has been lit by rush-light or neon.

"God Save the Queen!" "Soldiers of the Queen." "Gentlemen, the Queen!" The words move and inspire as no other heartfelt prayer, proud catch-phrase, or loyal toast could. They conjure up all the glories and traditions of the past upon the foundation of which lies the promise of the future; a future built with the same boldness and vigour, the same steadfastness and stability. It is to the Sovereign that the Government turns in time of emergency to unite the country into a national fervour capable of yielding the final ounce of effort and endurance, and of mollifying personal tragedy and disaster.

CHAPTER 12

THE CROWN AND THE COMMONWEALTH

WERE it not for the Queen, relations between Britain and each Commonwealth country would have to be defined by treaty and agreement. There is no written constitution for the Commonwealth, any more than there is for the United Kingdom. Freedom is the keynote of the Commonwealth—freedom to belong to the brotherhood, freedom to owe allegiance to the Crown, freedom to separate and become an independent foreign country if one wishes.

On being given self-government, Burma elected to leave the Commonwealth, and it was the United Kingdom that passed the Burma Independence Act, 1947, formally severing her relationship, just as in 1949 the Ireland Act satisfied Eire's desire to break off all ties. There is no compulsion on membership of the Commonwealth; no question of any enforced allegiance to the Crown. In fact, when India, on gaining independence, desired to remain within the Commonwealth and yet become a republic, provision was accordingly made.

In the case of India, allegiance to Queen Elizabeth is no longer the binding factor; but she still remains the essential link as the " symbol of the free association of its independent members and as such the Head of the Commonwealth ".

With other member nations, particularly those like Canada and Australia, which spring largely from British stock and look upon Britain as the " Old Country " or " Mother Country ", there is no foundation for believing that anything other than allegiance to the Queen would hold them to the United Kingdom. In 1937 Mr. Lapointe, Canadian Minister of Justice, said in the Federal Parliament of Canada :

" I desire to say today that the British Throne is the cement, the bond that unites all of us, and if it should disappear and be replaced by some other form, I am afraid that the end of the British Empire would be in sight and that Canada would soon not be part of the British Commonwealth of Nations."

It was Mr. Lapointe, then Canada's Minister of Marine, who in 1923 had first established a Dominion's right to act directly under the Crown and independent of any British minister. The occasion was a treaty between Canada and the United States for the purpose of protecting the halibut fisheries in the North Pacific. On the grounds that the matter affected Canada only, and was no concern of the Imperial Parliament, Mr. Lapointe refused to allow the presence of the British ambassador to Washington at the discussions. By-passing the United Kingdom parliament completely, he obtained the assent of the Crown, and signed with full powers on behalf of King George V.

Already in the young Queen Elizabeth's reign Australia and New Zealand have demonstrated that it is to her alone that they are responsible. They refused to invite representatives of the British Parliament to their discussions with the United States on the question of defence measures in the Pacific.

In the unique relationship that Queen Elizabeth bears between the various independent members of the Commonwealth it is possible that she may be offered different advice in different countries. Queen Elizabeth is powerless to act for the whole Commonwealth in unison. In a state of emergency, for instance, she could find herself proclaiming war in one part of the Commonwealth and a state of neutrality in another. In the last war, although the United Kingdom declared war against Germany on September 3, 1939, it was not until September 10 that, on the advice of his Canadian ministers, King George VI declared a state of war between Canada and Germany, while Eire, which at the time was still bound by the last tie of allegiance to the Crown, remained neutral for the duration of the conflict.

In domestic matters of trade or emigration, in which two or more Commonwealth countries are concerned, it is possible that Queen Elizabeth might find herself offered conflicting advice by her respective ministers. Should such a situation arise, there is no doubt that the Queen would then fulfil a vital rôle as mediator, using her personal influence to draw her conflicting ministers together and help them to find agreement.

Although personal monarchy, in the sense of direct personal government by the sovereign, died with George I, in another sense the monarchy has become more personal than ever, both at home and throughout the Commonwealth. Through press, photographs, radio, television, and films, Queen Elizabeth is already better known as a person to her peoples than any other sovereign. Every important event of her life, through childhood, her coming-of-age, her marriage, her motherhood, her accession, has been followed with proud interest, and shared with a sense of family closeness and intimacy by her subjects.

" Our ancient monarchy renders inestimable service to our country and to all the British Empire and Commonwealth of Nations," declared Mr. Churchill in the House of Commons in November 1948. " Above the ebb and flow of party strife, the rise and fall of ministries and individuals, the change of public opinion or of public fortune, the British monarchy presides, ancient, calm and supreme within its functions, over all the treasures that have been saved from the past and all the glories we write in the annals of our country. . . ."

Those glories cannot be written, it is obvious, by Queen Elizabeth alone. As Princess Elizabeth, the Queen made it clear that her twenty-first birthday vow of dedication to the service of ourselves and the " great imperial family to which we all belong " was possible only if the people themselves shared in it. Her throne must find its foundation in the hearts of her subjects, if the burden of monarchy is to be made bearable for her and her functions as Sovereign are to have a real and practical value.

I would like to adapt some lines that Tennyson wrote " To the Queen " to provide a particularly appropriate toast for Queen Elizabeth the Second— Elizabeth, Our Queen—and the future that lies before her.

> " Her court be pure ; her life serene,
> God give her peace ; her land repose ;
> A thousand claims to reverence close
> In her as Mother, Wife, and Queen."

So let it be.

ACKNOWLEDGMENTS

Among many authorities and references, I should like particularly to acknowledge the help I received, in preparing the outline of the Crown's part in the Constitution, from the following books:

A King's Story, H.R.H. the Duke of Windsor, K.G.; *Constitutional Law*, E. C. S. Wade and G. Godfrey Phillips; *The Law and Custom of the Constitution*, Sir William R. Anson; *Cabinet Government*, Sir W. Ivor Jennings; *This Realm of England*, Sir John Marriott; *The English King*, Michael Macdonagh; *The King and the Imperial Crown*, A. Berriedale Keith; *Crown, People and Parliament*, William Edwards; *Crown of England*, Erskine of Marr; *Constitutional History of England*, George Burton Adams; *Thoughts on the Constitution*, the Rt. Hon. L. S. Amery.

For permission to include the photographs in this book, the author and publishers are grateful to Camera Press, Central Press, Fox Photos, Topical Press and Dorothy Wilding.